An Illustrated
World History

J. M. Roberts was educated in Somerset and at
Keble College, Oxford. From 1953 to 1979 he
was a Fellow and Tutor in Modern History of
Merton College, Oxford. During that time he
paid several visits to the United States, and
held visiting professorships at the Universities
of South Carolina and Columbia. He edited
the extremely successful partwork publica-
tion, Purnell's *History of the Twentieth
Century*; and in 1976 brought out his one-
volume *History of the World* to great acclaim.
In 1979 he was appointed Vice-Chancellor of
Southampton University.

An Illustrated
World History
2

Design: Arthur Lockwood
Illustration research: Diana Phillips
Text research: Nicola Sissons

J. M. Roberts

The First Civilizations

Book Club Associates   London

Introduction

This volume deals with one of the biggest steps in human development, the appearance of the first civilizations. They are the real beginning of history. They made possible a quite new kind of existence for large numbers of human beings, offering scope for breaking with the age-old routines of prehistory. Yet it is very hard to be sure just exactly how this change came about. It is a little like the coming of agriculture. We might say that men 'discovered' civilization, or 'invented' it, or simply 'created' it unconsciously, according to what side of it we want to stress. Whatever words are used, the coming of civilization was a very complicated business, the result of many different changes all interacting.

Only the most important of such changes can be considered in this book. One way of looking at them is to take in turn the earliest examples of civilizations. Of most of them there is now little left except memories and ruins. Yet some of them still influence us, though often in ways we are scarcely aware of – through the enduring beliefs of great religions, for example, or through traditions and customs, or even through our techniques of writing or measuring. To understand this influence we need to study the development of these civilizations. The easiest place to start to do this is in the ancient land of Mesopotamia.

This edition published 1980 by
Book Club Associates
By arrangement with Penguin Books Ltd

Copyright © 1980 by J. M. Roberts

Design and illustration research by IKON
25 St Pancras Way, London NW1

First published 1980

Phototypeset by
Oliver Burridge & Co. Ltd, Crawley

Printed in Great Britain by
Hazell Watson & Viney Ltd, Aylesbury, Bucks

Contents

Title-page pictures: representations of faces from ancient civilizations. Left to right, Indian, Egyptian, Olmec (Mexico) and Minoan (Crete).

Mesopotamia

Mesopotamia is an ancient Greek name for what is now Iraq, and it was still in use about fifty years ago. It means 'land between two rivers'. Those rivers are the Tigris and Euphrates – two more very old names – and the big broad valley they run through has long been a place where human beings have lived. All round it lie high plateaux and mountains; the valley itself is pretty flat. Nowadays the Tigris and Euphrates run into the sea about 160 kilometres farther south than the coast lay 6000 or so years ago. 'Coast', though, is a word which is a little misleading, because the mouths of these rivers were – and still are – a great delta of marshes, mudbanks, creeks and inlets with a shifting edge to it. The map is constantly changing, but the mouths of the rivers have always tended to move southwards as the rivers

slowly bring down great masses of mud from the high valleys.

This was a rich soil. Southern Mesopotamia, or Sumer, as it was called in ancient times, was an easy place – one of the easiest, in fact – to grow crops, once men had discovered how to practise agriculture. There were other easily available sources of food too, in the fish and marsh-fowl which abounded in the delta. On the other hand, there were difficulties about living there. The sun was hot and summer wind-storms were violent. Perhaps the worst danger was flood; after the rainy season the rivers carried down huge quantities of water from the hills, which must time and time again have swept away the reed huts and little patches of cereal crops grown by the first people who lived there.

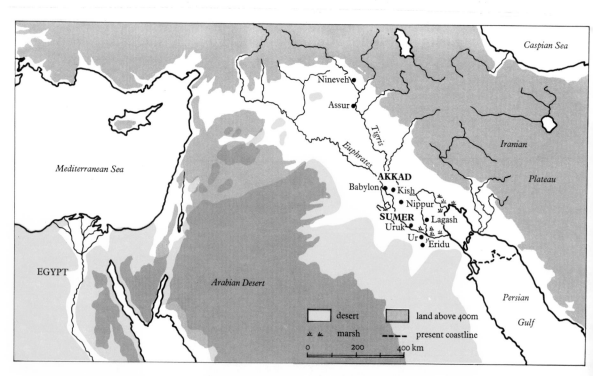

Modern Iraq – or ancient Sumer? Some things have not much changed in thousands of years. In the marshes of the lower Tigris (above) people still live in little villages of reed huts like those of the first Sumerians.

No one knows where these people came from, but they were already distinct from neighbouring peoples by about 4000 BC. They spoke a language which shows they were closely related neither to those who lived across the Tigris to the north, in the foothills of the Iranian plateau, nor to those who lived in the deserts to the south.

By 4000 BC many Sumerians already lived in communities like big villages, which had begun to try to do something about the challenges of flood and climate. Some of them had been established for hundreds of years. Later Mesopotamians had legends about the way the world was made which were handed down by these ancestors. They told how it had been made by the gods out of a watery waste (even people, it was believed, had been stamped out of mud like clay dolls). This is an interesting story, because, so far as we are able to tell, ancient Sumer was indeed 'made' in this way, but by the Sumerians themselves.

What seems to have happened is that marsh was gradually turned into agricultural land. Very slowly, over the centuries, the Sumerians dug channels to let flood water run away without doing damage, and they piled up mud and reed banks to make raised fields (much as, with more advanced tools and methods, the Dutch have been doing for the last five centuries or so). The more people who could be persuaded to cooperate in this way, the faster the making of new fields would go. Because of this, large villages had advantages no individual family could possess. But cooperative efforts have to rest on agreement about ways of doing things and about who should give orders. Out of this agreement came the first rulers and the first laws of which we have any knowledge.

The early stages of all this are very obscure. But evidence suggests that many things which had perhaps been going on elsewhere in a more elementary way for thousands of years – agriculture, metal-working, pottery,

This clay-tablet is a map of farmland near the city of Nippur made in about 1300 BC. The parallel lines show the networks of canals for irrigation and the owner of each plot is named.

The Sumerians liked to set up columns or 'steles' to celebrate important events. Sometimes they have pictures carved on them. This one shows an empty war-chariot. When it was carved, in about 2200 BC, spoked wheels had not been invented.

the building of religious shrines – came together in quite a new fashion in about 3500 BC and, as a result, people began living in a very different and much more complicated way from their ancestors. Some of the big villages became cities.

We know that some Sumerian kings had at different times authority extending over many of these cities. Their soldiers look as if they are wearing a sort of uniform of kilts and leather caps and seem to be commanded by generals who trundle about in four-wheeled cars drawn by asses. There were also stewards and civil servants. At the beginning many of these officials were probably priests because, in the earliest evidence we have of any sort of writing, it seems to be used to record the delivery of foodstuffs to temples.

This is still a topic about which we do not know very much, but it is clear that something we can call 'government' came about first in Sumer. However the Sumerians ran their affairs, they were not like most of the primitive peoples who still hunted and gathered their food in little tribal groups all over the world in ancient times. What may have happened in Sumer is that farmers had to hand over crops (a kind of taxation) to the temples (which were like government departments) for them to be doled out again to workers and their families instead of wages. But we cannot be sure about this. As for a long time they had no money, though, we can at least be sure that the ancient Mesopotamians' life was very unlike our own.

Yet they had some things in common with us that mark us and them off from their predecessors, from many of their contemporaries and even from some of ours. They had, for example, complicated laws. They played musical instruments and enjoyed board games. Above all, they had a literature. There are original texts from ancient Sumer, partly difficult to understand. Copies were later made of these great stories by men who admired them and wrote them down, or rewrote them, or copied Sumerian texts which have now disappeared. All this happened in the 1000 years or so after they begin to emerge from the mists of the fourth millennium BC. The Sumerians came a long way in that time. The short name for what they achieved is civilization. Sumer was the place where civilization first appeared and history (as opposed to prehistory) began. The rest of this book is about what followed, about the ways in which for 2000 or so years civilizations appeared in many other parts of the world. These things took place long ago, but much about the world in which we now live only makes sense if we understand what they left behind.

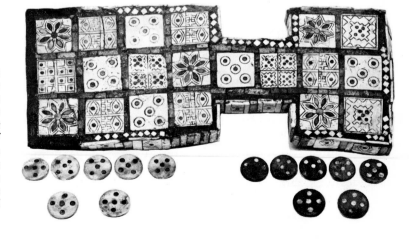

A board and counters for a Sumerian game. Other games somewhat like this seem to have been played in the east as far away as Sri Lanka, and in what was later Syria to the west. The staff of the British Museum, where this board can now be seen, have worked out rules for a game which can be played on it, though we cannot be sure it is the one played by Sumerians.

What is civilization?

It is a good idea to try to be clear at the outset about what the word 'civilization' means. Curiously, though we use it a lot, it is not an easy word to agree about. Scholars can still disagree about whether or not a particular society should be thought to have reached 'civilization'.

There is one thing, though, on which there is agreement: civilization is an 'advanced' or 'developed' state of society. It is something which has grown to a higher stage than what went before it. We may not be able to pin down exactly just *how far* a society has to have advanced, or *how much* it must have developed, in order to be called civilization, but we can at least agree that it is quite different from anything that could be called a primitive society.

Some people have tried to provide precise tests of civilization. They have said, for example, that civilization occurs when people begin to write things down – with literacy, in fact. Others have said that it is marked by a certain kind of technology – building in stone or brick, for example, and using these materials for big buildings which are meant like monuments to outlast those who built them and to serve more than just their simple daily needs. Still other people who have studied these matters say that you have a civilization when there are lots of people – potters, builders, smiths, jewellers – doing very specialized work and therefore relying for their food on other specialists (farmers and fishermen).

The trouble with all such tests (and many more have been suggested) is that it is almost always possible to find something we want to call a 'civilization' which nonetheless lacks one of these things. So it is probably safer to say that a civilization is very likely to show many of these features though none of them is absolutely essential.

Civilizations are complicated. They mix together all sorts of activities and make it possible for them to be carried on at a much higher level than in primitive societies. Technology, for example, advances much more quickly in civilized communities. The specialization and cooperation which many activities require are only possible because there is more wealth to share out. Somehow more food is produced to support large numbers of workers doing things other than growing food. This, of course, is why the coming of agriculture was probably the most important change in the whole human story until only a few hundred years ago. It made civilization possible.

For one thing, more food meant more people. It is very hard to do more than make highly approximate estimates, but it does seem that the whole world in 4000 BC contained about eighty or ninety million people. This is not many to modern eyes – it is about half the population of the modern Soviet Union – but it is enormous by comparison with earlier times. It was to take the next 4000 years or so to rise to about 130 million and this too is not much in modern terms. Yet it was a much faster rate of growth than anything earlier.

One mark of the appearance of civilizations is that more people live in cities. This gathering together of people in larger groups is another sign of an important change. The word 'civilization' itself reflects it, for it is taken from a Latin word *civis* which means 'citizen' or someone who lives in a city. Early cities were not very big by our standards. Nor do most people in the world live in cities, even now. Nonetheless the coming together of people in larger numbers in cities, where they could learn from one another and see new and unfamiliar things, made civilization easier.

Once a civilization has appeared, it has a huge effect on people. It is always worth remembering that, for almost all the time that human beings have existed, the vast majority of them have had very little choice about anything important. In the earliest times (and still in certain corners of the earth) geography and climate forced human life into rigid patterns. When agriculture and civilization appeared, a few more people had a little more choice open to them. Even so, for most of human history, most young people have had no choice about what they would do when they grew up.

While civilization freed men in some ways, it laid new restraints on them in others. It made it easier to develop skills and ways of doing things which gave men power over nature, but civilization also reinforced traditions. Most civilizations lasted for centuries. This gave time for their ways of thinking and behaving to become very strongly established and hard to change. We still find it difficult to understand the thinking of people from other traditions than our own.

The Pagan people of northern Nigeria live in villages of mud huts (above). These huts are obviously not built to last as long as the ancient Egyptian obelisk and colossi of Ramses II (right) have done. To some people this means the ancient Egyptians were civilized, while the contemporary Pagans remain primitive.

The first civilizations

We do not know exactly how civilizations first appeared. Once some civilizations were already in existence, they then tended to pass on to other areas knowledge and skills which made it easier for civilization to appear in them too.

No one now believes (as some scholars once did) that everything we think of as fundamental to civilization was invented first in one place and was then passed on so as to start up new civilizations elsewhere. Although there may have been slight contacts between some of them, it seems that civilization was 'invented', or 'occurred' (whichever is the right word), in at least six places which were for a very long time for all practical purposes independent of one another.

Sumerian or Mesopotamian civilization was the oldest. It was established by about 3500

BC. Soon afterwards another civilization appeared in the Near East, that of ancient Egypt. Another flourished in India by about 2500 BC, but one in Crete whose shape first became clear in about 2000 BC may have overlapped with it in time. China had her first civilization by about 1500 BC. The only other example we need consider of a civilization appearing quite independently was in Central America. This was much later still, probably in about 800 BC.

There is an obvious question: what did the areas in which these first civilizations appeared have in common? Do they explain why things took the turn they did there and not elsewhere?

As the map shows, they were scattered all round the world's northern hemisphere. They were not to be found either in the coldest or hottest regions. Six or seven thousand years

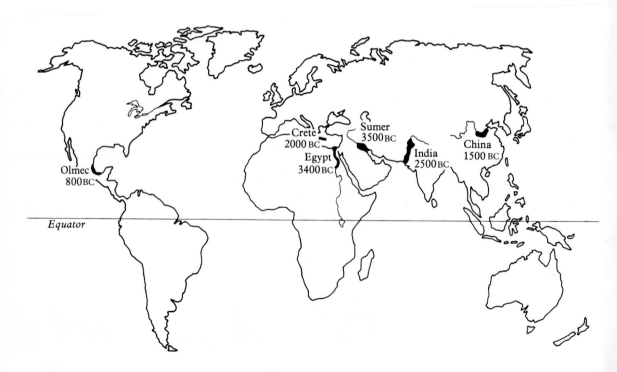

Crete 2000 BC
Sumer 3500 BC
Egypt 3400 BC
India 2500 BC
China 1500 BC
Olmec 800 BC
Equator

ago, too, the climate was milder and wetter in the Near East than it is now; and the north-west corner of India was not then the desert much of it is today, but was wooded and green. Four of these areas, too, were great river valleys: Mesopotamia, the Nile, the Indus and the Yellow River valleys all had rich soil, easily worked. These were areas where agriculture was easy and population could grow fairly rapidly.

This is probably – it is best not to be too definite – the main reason why civilization appears first in these places. Gradually, in the right agricultural setting, numbers of little villages built up into bigger units – small towns – which made men think of more complicated and large-scale ways of doing things. Once they found suitable food crops for the climate (as they did), the Indian peoples of Central America could multiply on the rich soils of their semi-tropical forests, too. Only Crete seems not to have had the advantage of rich agricultural land. But the Cretans had other advantages – a fine central position in a sea of islands with access to the great civilizations of the Near East and Egypt.

The appearance of the later civilizations is much less difficult to explain than that of the earliest ones. From Mesopotamia, for example, influences spread outwards, which produced civilizations which had a lot in common all over the Near East by 1000 BC. Indian civilization eventually had a sphere of influence covering Asia and Indonesia, while Chinese civilization came to dominate a huge area in the Far East. The Central American civilizations, on the other hand, remained confined by geography; they could not penetrate the barriers it imposed on them.

Yet for a long time only a small area was really covered by any of the first civilizations. They existed for hundreds of years without much influence on one another. The isolation of the Central Americans from other civilized regions was simply the most complete.

Sheer muscle-power was all that the ancient engineer could call on for his greatest works. This nineteenth-century drawing of an Egyptian stone carving shows how a huge statue was moved from the quarry where it had been carved. No cart could carry it because no axle could be made strong enough. It had to be dragged on a sledge.

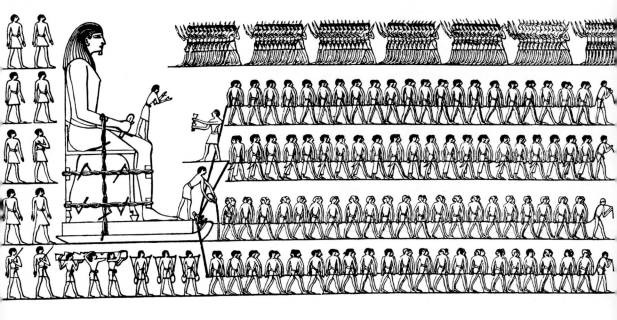

Later Sumer

Against this general background, we can now look a little more closely at Sumer and the story of ancient Mesopotamia. It conveniently divides into two parts. There is the story of Sumer and a distinctive Sumerian culture which lasts about 1300 years – from 3300 to 2000 BC is a close enough dating. After this comes a much more confused period, lasting until about 1000 BC. During this time the old river valley was increasingly a theatre of conflicts between peoples drawn into it from a much larger area. The Near East was by then beginning to fill up with kingdoms and empires, some civilized, some half-civilized, who often shared ways and skills first learnt from Mesopotamia.

During the first 900 years or so of Sumerian history, the Sumerians lived in cities ruled by kings. Some of these cities had very old roots:

The oldest town plan in the world: Nippur, on the Euphrates, shown on a clay tablet of about 1500 BC. The river runs up the left-hand side of the city; on the far right is a square building which was the shrine of the city's chief god.

they were often ancient religious sites, where, in prehistoric times, there had been shrines or temples visited by people from many surrounding villages. One such place, Eridu, has been traced back to about 5000 BC. Sumerian tradition said it was the first city to be founded by the gods.

By 3500 BC Eridu was a small town of 4000 or so people, on a site of about ten hectares. In the next 1000 years cities grew much larger than this. In 3000 BC another city, Ur, had about 24,000 inhabitants (as many as modern Durham) and covered almost 120 hectares. Other cities grew larger still.

Most Sumerians were farmers. This would have been true of about four fifths of those at Ur, though as time went by they drew increasingly on the services of specialists for things they did not make themselves. Each town was the centre of a cultivated district and even poor men seem to have been likely to own their own small plots for kitchen-gardening. We know this because early laws tell us that the rich and powerful were likely to try to take over such small-holdings for themselves. These plots, together with houses scattered in the fields and much waste ground inside the city, must have given Sumerian cities a rather untidy appearance but helped to make them self-sufficient for much of their early history. For the most part, they lay along the Euphrates or along the canals which increasingly criss-crossed Sumer and gave it internal lines of communication. Between them there was usually marshy country not reclaimed and difficult to work.

The first Mesopotamians had lived in reed huts, later covered in mud. Stone was always scarce in Sumer and so other materials had to be sought when more permanent dwellings were needed. The answer was found again in the mud which was the ultimate foundation

of all Sumerian life – but it was mud made into bricks.

The first bricks were simply dried in the hot Mesopotamian sun. The earliest temple discovered at Eridu – a tiny one, only three metres square – was made of them. Yet, though this suggests that such bricks could last a long time, houses built of sun-dried brick were always liable to collapse (there is much about this in Sumerian law, too). Still, they provided cheap material: only rich people could afford bricks baked hard by fire, for fuel was expensive. Most Sumerians lived in little dried brick houses, with thick walls to keep out the heat, low doors and the few windows stopped with clay or wooden grilles.

A stone drinking-trough from Sumer is decorated with this picture (above) of a goat-pen made from reeds. The odd-looking pointed object is a garland showing the place was sacred. Below: a Sumerian banquet and animals being taken to the king as tribute.

Private houses had no drainage, but by the middle of the third millennium BC there were big official buildings with properly built drains and cess-pools made of baked bricks. Such buildings were the first to have true arches – something the Sumerians seem to have invented – and were sometimes decorated with bands of coloured clay cones sticking out from the walls which threw patterns of shadow. These buildings were sometimes supported by large pillars of brick.

The biggest and most highly decorated buildings of all were temples. There is a temple at Uruk of about 3500 BC, built on a terrace faced with baked brick, which is twelve metres high – it has been calculated that building it would have needed the work of 1500 men for five years. Work on this scale – like that of the efforts needed for big irrigation and canal works – suggests that Sumerian rulers could mobilize large resources when they needed to do so and that the Sumerians were always especially ready to make efforts to build for the gods.

They believed these gods lived in high places – the remote mountains which few Sumerians ever saw but which some scholars have thought to be their place of origin. Mountains may have been commemorated in the towering *ziggurats*, the terraced temples which dominated the Mesopotamian plain. No doubt they were first built in order to raise the shrine of a local god above flood water, but the Sumerians went on to pile up huge structures and came to believe that the gods lived at the top of them. The story of the Tower of Babel in the Old Testament is probably based on someone's memory of a *ziggurat*.

For many centuries, the Sumerian cities kept much to themselves, fighting one another occasionally – often, it seems, over some question of irrigation. Their kings saw themselves as 'stewards' of the gods, on whose behalf they governed men, and some of them established dynasties: hereditary monarchy had arrived.

From time to time their cities were troubled by neighbouring peoples. There was a tendency, as Sumer grew richer, for mountain folk and desert nomads to press upon it. The surrounding peoples for the most part belonged to a family of tribes now called 'Semitic', because they all spoke languages which belong to the same group. Arabic and Hebrew are the best-known Semitic languages still spoken today. The Sumerians belonged to a different linguistic group – the Caucasian.

Between 2400 and 2350 BC (dates are becoming more exact) a king of one of these Semitic peoples established himself at Akkad, to the north of Sumer, and from there conquered all

The ancient Mesopotamians were very good at making little · engraved seals from cylinders of hard stone. The scenes shown on them tell us a lot about the ancient world. They were rolled on to a strip of clay, which was thus impressed with a picture like this one from a seal made in about 2250 BC, showing a mythological scene, the liberation of the sun-god from the earth.

The greatest building at Ur was the huge ziggurat built by a king in about 2100 BC. It went on being venerated and used for 1,500 years. Nothing now remains of the temple of the moon-god which once stood on top of it, but its huge walls of fired brick (the base was 60 by 40 metres) have been restored so that its original appearance can easily be understood and it is shown in this drawing.

the Sumerian cities. His name was Sargon and he was the first of many great conquerors in Near Eastern history. If half of what is reported of him is true, he must have been an amazing man for his time. He is supposed to have ruled lands stretching from Palestine to the Persian Gulf, to have invaded Egypt and even Ethiopia. Five thousand soldiers, it was boasted, ate at Sargon's expense in his palace.

All this, true or not, matters less here than the fact, which is not disputed, that Sargon was the first king to join Sumer to northern Mesopotamia in one big state and to give it common government. Later kings called themselves 'King of Sumer and Akkad'. His was the first unified empire in history and the first political unity covering the whole Mesopotamia valley, though it did not last beyond his great-grandson. Soon after 2200 the Akkadian empire was overthrown by mountain peoples from the north-east. This allowed the old Sumerian tradition to thrive again, with different cities at different times exercising a sort of overlordship over the rest.

The most successful was Ur. Under its kings Sumerian civilization had a final blaze of splendour. The later royal tombs of Ur reveal that it was a period of great wealth; destroyed temples were rebuilt on a bigger and better scale. This will not, of course, have changed the life of the ordinary farmer much.

A copper head which may be a portrait of the great Sargon of Akkad. The map, 1700 years later, illustrates the tale of his conquests, written out above it.

Finally, Sumerian civilization went under in about 2000 BC before another wave of invaders from the outside. Yet it did not quite disappear. In thirteen centuries the Sumerians had done much that could not be obliterated. They left behind the first writing; the art of monumental building; an ideal of abstract justice expressed in a set of laws; a number of religious ideas which are still shaping people's lives today; the invention of glass-making; much practical knowledge of irrigation; the first potter's turntable; a knowledge of brewing; the first portraits in the history of art; a way of counting in units of sixty, which is still the foundation of our measurement of time and of circles; and the idea that a number's value can be represented by its position as well as by its form (for example, I can stand for I or 10 or many other things according to where it is placed in relation to a decimal point).

It is an impressive legacy from the first society to produce a civilization.

Some early Mesopotamian statues, like this couple from Nippur, are very appealing, though not very lifelike. The statue of a king, Gudea of Lagash, is much more recognizable. It can be compared with several others of him, for he presided over his city at a time when it was obviously a great artistic centre, in about 2100 BC.

Royal tombs at Ur

In 1922 a British archaeologist, Leonard Woolley, began to excavate the ancient city of Ur. Almost at once he made wonderful discoveries. Over the next twelve years, his work and that of other scholars added enormously to what was known about southern Mesopotamia, but what really caught the attention of the world was the unearthing of a series of fine tombs, seventeen of them with unusually rich contents. They were soon named 'the Royal Tombs', and although this may not be strictly correct, they were clearly the burial places of very distinguished people who could afford costly possessions, some of which are shown here.

One of a pair of he-goats feeding from a tree, made from wood and covered in hammered gold and silver.

An example of what careful restoration can do : the head-dress and jewellery shown on the dummy were made from the fragments around the crushed skull in the left-hand picture, and show what a Sumerian lady would have worn.

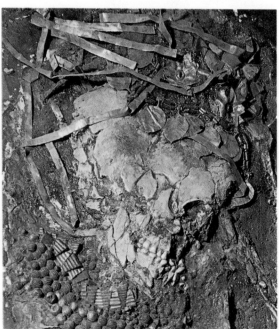

This bull's head (left) formed part of a harp which had crumbled away, though its shape could be reconstructed (below) from marks left in the sand. Elsewhere, there was a picture of a man playing a lyre (above).

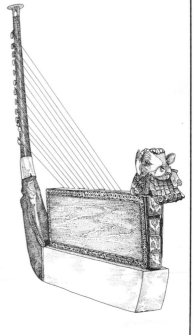

A gold helmet, beaten from a single sheet of metal, which belonged to a prince. It was placed on his head after death and was found crushed in his tomb.

Ancient Egypt

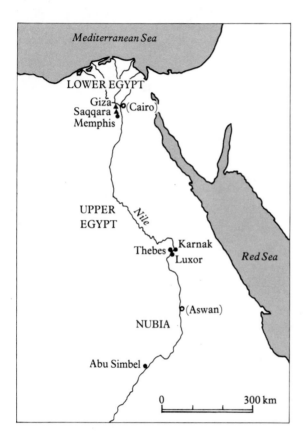

Soon after it appeared in Sumer, civilization started to develop in Egypt. The Egyptians may have learnt from Sumer, but we do not know exactly how, what, or to what extent. It was probably more important that, as in Sumer, agriculture was easy in Egypt in very early times. This was because of the water of the River Nile and the fertile mud deposited along its banks.

In prehistory, changes in climate had led gradually to the drying up of most of Egypt outside the valley of the Nile itself. Yet the narrow strip it provided – 1100 kilometres or so long, and anything from six to twenty kilometres wide – was (and still is) immensely fertile. A great many people could live there. On the banks of mud built up since prehistoric times, when the valley had been just a broad marsh hundreds of kilometres long, the first Egyptians were able to start farming. Egypt eventually became a long, straggling oasis surrounded by desert and rock.

This sounds something like the story of ancient Mesopotamia, yet there were big differences between it and Egypt. To begin with, the Nile was a much friendlier river than the

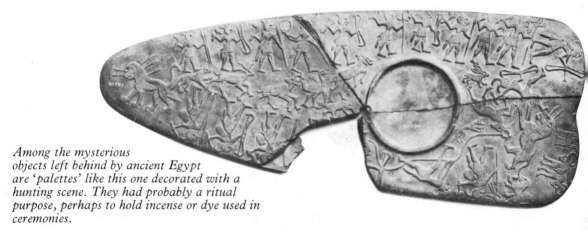

Among the mysterious objects left behind by ancient Egypt are 'palettes' like this one decorated with a hunting scene. They had probably a ritual purpose, perhaps to hold incense or dye used in ceremonies.

Tigris and Euphrates. Although it too would flood each year, overflowing its banks and washing away or burying in mud what stood on them, it did this very predictably. Its floods were not the sudden, surprising disasters of the Mesopotamian delta, but regular – so regular, in fact, that they set the pattern of the agricultural year. The Nile was a huge clock which regulated the life of ancient Egyptians by giving it a basic rhythm that went on without varying year after year.

People lived along its lower length in villages and communities not much separated from one another and, at the outset of historical

One of the first documents of Egyptian history is a palette depicting on its two sides the unification of Egypt by King Narmer (his legendary name was Menes). The great king is shown larger than the human figures in the design. On one side he wears the white crown of his own land; on the other the red crown of the land he conquered.

White crown of Upper (South) Egypt.

Red crown of Lower (North) Egypt.

Double crown.

Even today, a picture of the Nile can give a vivid sense of the difference between the narrow agricultural strip it watered and the surrounding desert. Ancient Egyptian art is full of river-life – from the busy agricultural scene below to the baby hippo above.

times – about 3300 BC – they seem to have thought of themselves as members of different clans, not as people living in different cities. Cities did not develop on the Nile as they did elsewhere until thousands of years had passed. One reason for this may have been that for a long time ancient Egypt had few neighbours who might threaten her people and force them to live in towns for their protection.

About the origin of civilization in Egypt much is still unknown because each year the Nile washed away great quantities of our evidence, or buried it deep in the banks of soil which slowly rose above high-water mark as the centuries passed. Once civilization has taken root there, though, we have almost at once a lot of information. This is because the Egyptians had from the start a form of writing, called 'hieroglyph'. A series of very old hieroglyphic inscriptions tell us the outline of the story of ancient Egypt. This account is probably not very far from the truth.

We learn of an Egypt already organized in two kingdoms, northern and southern, at the end of the fourth millennium BC. Soon, the records say, a great king from the south called Menes conquered the north. The result was a single kingdom some 1000 kilometres long ruled from Memphis. This was a much bigger affair than any of the city-states of Sumer of that time, though it is very hard to judge the real power of such a 'state'. Still, it is impressive even to claim to have governed so big an area. For the next 2000 or so years Egypt lived largely under one ruler, one religious system and one pattern of government, without any important influence from the outside breaking in to change things. This was taken for granted as the proper state of affairs.

All the same, ancient Egypt had its ups and downs. The state was sometimes strong and prosperous, sometimes weak and poor. These ups and downs, together with the fact that Egyptian historical records are very plentiful

Fowl – wild and domestic – were very important sources of food in the marshes of the Nile valley. Egyptian artists observed them with great accuracy, and clearly loved to depict them.

Ancient Egypt : time chart

Date BC	Dynasty	
3110-2665	**Predynastic Period**	
3110-2884	Dynasty I	Upper and Lower Egypt united by Menes with Memphis as capital
2883-2665	Dynasty II	
2664-2155	**Old Kingdom**	
2664-2615	Dynasty III	Pyramid building Step pyramid c. 2650
2614-2502	Dynasty IV	Pyramid of Cheops at Giza c. 2575
2501-2342	Dynasty V	
2341-2181	Dynasty VI	
2180-2175	Dynasty VII	
2174-2155	Dynasty VIII	
2154-2052	**Intermediate Period**	
2154-c. 2100	Dynasty IX	Internal strife,
2100-2052	Dynasty X	decline in prosperity and arts
2134-1999	Dynasty XI	Reunification of Egypt with Thebes as capital
2051-1786	**Middle Kingdom**	
1991-1786	Dynasty XII	
1785-1553	**Intermediate Period**	
1785-1550	Dynasties XIII-XVI	Hyksos domination. They introduce new
c. 1715-c. 1650	Dynasty XIV	ideas and technology –
1652-1544	Dynasty XV	horse-drawn chariots,
c. 1600-1554	Dynasty XVII	improved weapons, spinning and weaving, new musical instruments
1554-1075	**New Kingdom**	
1554-1304	Dynasty XVIII	Akhnaton tries to introduce monotheism Tutankhamon (c.1358-1340)
1304-1192	Dynasty XIX	Ramses II (1290-1224) Temples of Karnak and Abu Simbel
1192-1075	Dynasty XX	Invasion of the 'Sea People'
1075-664	**Late Dynastic Period**	
1075-940	Dynasty XXI	
940-730	Dynasty XXII	
c. 761-715	Dynasty XXIII	
725-710	Dynasty XXIV	
736-657	Dynasty XXV	Assyrian invasions
664-525	Dynasty XXVI	
525-404	Dynasty XXVII	Persians rule Egypt
404-398	Dynasty XXVIII	
398-378	Dynasty XXIX	
378-341	Dynasty XXX	Last Egyptian pharaohs
341-333	Dynasty XXXI	Persians reconquer Egypt
332-30	**Greek Period**	
	Alexander the Great conquers Egypt	

and provide fairly precise facts and dates, have led scholars to talk about ancient Egypt in terms of three big divisions of time. There was the 'Old Kingdom', running from 2664 to 2155 BC, then a century or so of turmoil before the next, the 'Middle Kingdom', began in 2051. This lasted until 1786 BC, when another difficult period started which only came to an end with the beginning of the 'New Kingdom' in 1554 BC. (The diagram shows how the dates of dynasties or royal families, another way of dividing Egyptian history, fitted into this more general pattern.)

For the moment the Old Kingdom is all that need concern us. It is important because so much of what went on for the next 1500 years (and, in some matters, even longer) started then. One of the most obvious examples was the Egyptian tradition of large-scale building. The Old Kingdom erected the pyramids. These are some of the most famous monuments ever made (for centuries they were listed as one of the Seven Wonders of the World) and there can be few people who have not seen a picture of one, if only on a travel poster.

The first pyramids were huge tombs for kings. They were almost solid (the passages and rooms inside were very small in proportion to their bulk) and they required enormous amounts of labour. This was in part because they were so big – the biggest of them, at Giza, was nearly 170 metres high and contained nearly six million tonnes of stone – and in part because the Egyptians had only the most elementary equipment. Great slabs of stone had to be manhandled on sledges or rollers (they could build no axle strong enough for a wheeled cart to carry them) without windlasses, pulleys, or block and tackle. Such difficulties make the accuracy with which they were built all the more amazing. The pyramid of Cheops at Giza is exactly aligned with the points of the compass and rests on a rock foundation which does not vary more than twenty-five millimetres in elevation all round.

Each side of the base is over 250 metres long, but the difference between the longest and shortest is less than twenty centimetres.

Pyramids were suitable tombs for kings thought by the Egyptians to be gods. In this way too Egypt was unlike Mesopotamia. The notion that their rulers were divine may have come to the Egyptians through the idea that they controlled agriculture by making possible the annual flooding of the Nile. Kings believed to be rainmakers have been found in other parts of Africa at other times. Whether this is so or not, the Old Kingdom kings had greater authority than the priests. Soon they were worshipped as the descendants of gods and therefore as gods themselves.

In this way government and religion were closely mixed in ancient Egypt. The temples certainly had an important part to play in government, though it is difficult to be sure exactly what it was. But it seems to have had a lot to do with the organization, feeding and paying of the thousands of workmen who were assembled for the great building projects.

The great pyramids at Giza still dominate the banks of the Nile. Here (right) they are shown in floodtime. Another group of pyramids (at Abusir) is shown below, drawn as they would have looked when the long causeways linking them to the Nile were in place. Along these the bodies of the kings brought by water would have been carried to the tombs.

28

Though he died nearly four and a half thousand years ago, we can still see what the singer Wati looked like (above). He was buried in a tomb belonging to the family of a much more successful singer, who had risen through his skill to become an important official at Court. About him and his family we know much more than about Wati.

Tombs often contain much information about their builders and owners. Usually mummified bodies were placed in cases like the one containing the priestess from Thebes shown here (left) and these, too, were sometimes inscribed and richly decorated. Other information about the way the Egyptians thought about death comes from writings such as this papyrus, which shows (below) a soul being weighed by the gods while its fate is decided.

Models of the possessions of the dead were often put in their tombs with their bodies. This little house, made in clay, has food laid out in the courtyard.

A funeral boat, carrying a mummy under the central canopy. Most tombs had one of these, so that the soul could travel on pilgrimage after death.

These went on for centuries and have left behind a large number of monuments other than the pyramids. Most of them, though, are graves, or at least monuments to the dead. Kings and rich people built themselves and their families elaborate tombs, often beautifully decorated with paintings which tell us about daily life in Egypt. Stone was easier to find in Egypt than in Sumer, but expensive: ordinary people lived only in mud-brick or reed huts which soon perished, but we know something of their design because some of their features were later copied in stone.

After the pyramids, the most familiar object that has come down to us from ancient Egypt is the mummy case. This is really a box or coffin, decorated and shaped so as to remind people of the person whose embalmed body lay inside. Embalming was a skilled and complicated business, involving the removal of the insides of the dead person, the treating of the rest of the body with special preservatives and the wrapping of it carefully in bandages. The faces of some of the mummies are still intact: they tell us what men and women of thousands of years ago looked like. But this is probably because the hot, dry air of the desert stopped them decomposing, rather than because of the embalmers' skill.

Why were the Egyptians so fascinated by graves and death? A clue lies in their wish to preserve the dead as perfectly and in as lifelike a setting as possible. They buried people surrounded with household objects – beds, pots, jewellery, toys and tools. They were even given food. The reason was that the Egyptians thought men would live on after death in another world, providing they had not been so unlucky or so wicked as to have lost this chance. Other peoples have had similar ideas. What is curious about the Egyptians is the singlemindedness and keenness with which they concentrated on getting ready for the next world. Sometimes they seem more concerned with the next life than with this one.

India

'India' can mean two different things. One is the modern republic of that name, which has existed since 1947. The other is the whole of what is sometimes called the 'sub-continent', the roughly triangular peninsula which stretches from Kashmir to its tip in the Indian Ocean about 2400 kilometres to the south.

In this second sense, India is a huge place, containing many different landscapes and climates, many languages and peoples. This has been so for a very long time. About 5000 years ago it seems that dark-skinned peoples of a type called Dravidians, whose descendants are now found mainly in the south of India, were also to be found in the north. Perhaps they were the original Indians, but it is difficult to be sure, because many new peoples, invaders and immigrants, have entered that part of the sub-continent since very early times. They came through passes in the north-western mountains, which for thousands of years offered the only easy way into India by land; even India's links with China were for a long time by this route.

Some people think that Indian civilization was brought (or at least touched off) from the outside, by foreigners, because the first signs of it are to be found there in the north-west, in the valley of the Indus river-system. This was where agriculture started in India, where there is the first evidence of pottery being made on the wheel and where cotton was in use well before 2000 BC. By then there were cities too, though a long time after civilization had started in Mesopotamia and Egypt. So it seems possible that people from the outside brought to

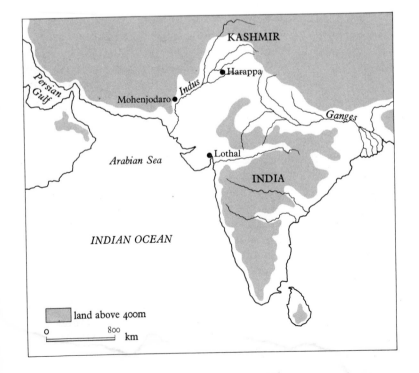

India skills which these early Indians took up. But no one can say with certainty. It may be, instead, that the Indians simply arrived at civilization for themselves, as the Mesopotamians had done.

Whatever the explanation, the first Indian civilization had appeared by about 2500 BC. The evidence for it is provided by archaeology: in thirty or forty different places in the Indus valley excavations have uncovered something of the story, though much is still unknown. The most remarkable discoveries were made at Mohenjodaro and Harappa, where the ruins of whole cities have been found.

These have told scholars a great deal. To begin with, they were big places, possibly even the biggest cities of their time. They covered hundreds of hectares and had walls about four kilometres round. They probably had about 35,000 inhabitants each. Such big cities show that agriculture must have been well developed and prosperous – and this, in turn, means that

there must have been ways of controlling the flooding of the Indus, with probably quite elaborate drainage and irrigation systems to support agriculture.

Such irrigation systems probably benefited from another feature of Mohenjodaro and Harappa: both cities are built (like many other relics of Indus civilization) from baked brick. Stone is not easy to come by in the Indus valley, but there was then plenty of wood to provide fuel to heat brick-kilns; the area was much more heavily forested in prehistoric times than it is today. Unlike sun-dried mud bricks, baked brick could be used for dams, culverts and canals which would last.

Whatever the explanation of the appearance of civilization in India, its first cities must have been impressive. Besides the official quarters, they had residential areas, laid out on a very regular grid-pattern, with main streets running north–south and smaller streets running into them east–west. The streets were not paved, so

Relics from the Indus cities: clay models of a woman or a goddess, a dog with a collar, a bullock-cart like those still used in Pakistan, and a monkey.

Mohenjodaro and Harappa must always have been dusty or muddy, according to the time of year, but they were very well provided for in other ways. Brick-lined sewers carried away water from bathrooms and latrines in each house. They had covered man-holes for cleaning and inspection. Rubbish-shoots from the houses collected other kinds of waste. Altogether, the cities of the Indus had very advanced sanitation. Large baths or tanks, like those in many Indian villages today, have also been discovered. Bathing is still a very important part of the ritual of Indian religion and it looks as if this goes back a very long way indeed.

Mohenjodaro and Harappa are about as far apart as London and Edinburgh. Other remains from their civilization are to be found over an area which stretches from the tributaries of the Ganges in the east, to the coast in the south. This is a much larger area than early Sumer and it suggests that someone was pro-

A view of the excavated city citadel at Mohenjo-daro, whose solid walls and drains of baked brick can clearly be seen.

viding some sort of government or general oversight of the region. We know, for example, that bricks of the same size – made, as it were, to official specification – were used throughout the entire region. Weights and measures, too, seem to have been standardized.

So far, scholars have not succeeded in reading the writing left behind by this civilization. It is to be found on thousands of seals which have survived, some of them very beautiful. They seem to have been used for marking bundles of goods. This, together with the regularity of weights and measures, makes it look as if there was a lot of trade in the Indus valley. Some of it was with other countries too: at Lothal, on the coast, there is a brick-lined dock nearly 250 metres long and thirty-five

The Indus valley seals were not cylindrical, like the Mesopotamian, but were flat stamps for impressing on clay. This curious one-horned beast appears on many of them, perhaps for religious reasons.

metres wide, connected to the river by a channel almost one and a half kilometres long. Big anchor-stones have been found there, which show it was used by large boats. Traces of the seals which were used for bundles of goods have turned up as far away as the top end of the Persian Gulf.

The Indus civilization came to an end within a couple of centuries after 2000 BC. One reason may have been the arrival from the north of new peoples, called 'Aryans' after the kind of language they spoke. They were entering India from about 2000 BC onwards. They had bronze weapons and, if they came into conflict with the peoples of the Indus cities, who had no metals, this would have given them a big advantage. Archaeologists have found skeletons at Mohenjodaro from about 1750 BC which look like those of men killed in battle.

But other explanations for the decline of Indus civilization have been suggested, too. The later buildings of the cities are much less regular and well ordered than those from earlier times, and this has been taken as a sign of a weakening government. There is a possibility too that the Indus cities used up so much of the forest and woodland for their brick-ovens and by clearing it for cultivation or pasture that they caused erosion and desiccation – a new climate, which was too dry to support agriculture on the necessary scale.

Human beings have often exploited their natural environment to the point at which it is irreparably damaged and this may be why the Indus civilization disappeared.

But we do not know. We can only say that there is still much more to discover about the first Indian civilization, though we already know that it was capable of great things in its heyday and could rival, in some respects, the civilizations of early Sumer and Egypt.

No one is quite sure whom this bearded figure from Mohenjodaro represents, but it is probably a priest. The pattern on his cloak turns up over much of the ancient east.

Civilization starts in China

China is a very large country, not easy to penetrate by land except from the north and much divided internally. It has three great rivers; one of them, the Hwang-Ho, is about 4300 kilometres long and rises in Mongolia to flow through north China to the sea. (The place where it comes out has changed many times in history, sometimes by hundreds of kilometres.) Because it brings down huge masses of yellowish silt from the mountains into the northern Chinese plain it is called the Yellow River. Chinese civilization first appeared on its banks.

North China in ancient times was probably much warmer than it is now (though it is still hot in summer; Peking is further south than Naples) and rhinoceros and elephants were still found there in about 1000 BC. For a long time, it drew immigrants from the deserts of Mongolia, which were becoming drier an colder. Across these deserts China was later make contact with India and the Near Eas Her own culture and civilization develope first in the north, then spread southwards ov thousands of years. Because of great mounta ranges and forests, southern China was alwa relatively inaccessible.

The prehistoric Chinese may have take some skills from peoples further west wh arrived at civilization at an earlier date, but th outcome was so distinctive that China's civ lization can be considered virtually home grown. Agriculture was practised in the Yello River valley earlier than 4000 BC. By about 15c BC the region contained many cities. The buildings do not survive, because they we built of wood (and, in the case of the comm

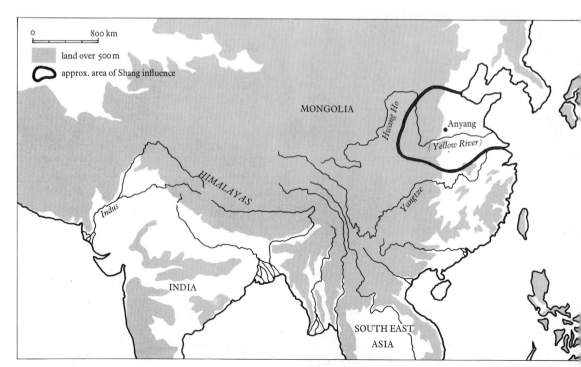

people's hovels, of mud), but we know their size and shape because the foundations of pounded earth survive. One city was about two and a half kilometres square and had a wall of pounded earth more than six metres high round it. The valley people had also progressed beyond any other part of the world in certain skills, notably in casting big bronze jars and vessels which were used for religious rituals. They did this by a distinctive method not used elsewhere until long after, casting each object in a single mould assembled from many pieces. They also knew how to grow silk from silkworms.

We know the Chinese had writing at this time because of the survival of 'oracle-bones' from which they sought guidance. An animal's shoulder-blade or a turtle shell was written on; then a little groove or hole was made in it

The Chinese characters on this tortoise shell explain how the cracks were interpreted.

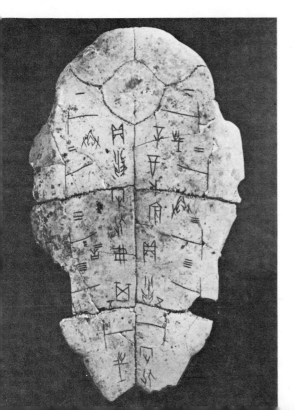

and heated so that cracks radiated outwards from it. From the pattern of the cracks the diviners then worked out the answers to questions they had put to the oracle.

After use, such records were usually filed away in the archives. They often had the dates and names of rulers on them, which enabled scholars to confirm much that was said in traditional Chinese histories (not written until many centuries later, of course) about the first Chinese state of which we know anything, ruled by a people called the Shang. The oracle-bones could be read because they were written in characters similar to those of modern Chinese; this showed that some ancient Chinese were already speaking and writing a language that is still in use today. Few European languages go back in a recognizable modern form more than 600 or 700 years; for an equivalent in modern Europe, we should all have to be speaking ancient Greek.

Language has helped to make the Chinese much more aware of the continuing life of their civilization than of the breaks in it. Since it has a continuity going back at least to 1500 BC, they are right to be proud of it. By 1000 BC, though China was still not the great empire she was later to become, many other things which were to be characteristic of Chinese life had made their appearance.

There was, for example, the very high standard of workmanship both in casting bronze and in making pottery which was to make Chinese art so much admired in other countries. At an equally early date the Chinese already attached enormous importance (as they were to continue to do) to the family as the main unit of society, and worshipped ancestors who were thought to intercede with the gods on behalf of the living. Another long-lasting feature which had appeared was the great gulf between the ordinary people and the noblemen, who had a special religious standing. The king himself was unique; he could carry out sacrifices no one else could undertake. On his

Bronze casting in China

This bronze container (of a kind called **Ting***) was made under the Shang. It was used in rituals, possibly for human remains sacrificed to ancestors, since it has human faces on it. But often such containers held only food offerings.*

The container was made from a mould made up of several sections. The diagram (below left) shows the four outside and the two core sections. The mould was assembled and turned upside down ready to receive the molten metal (below right). This process was unique to China.

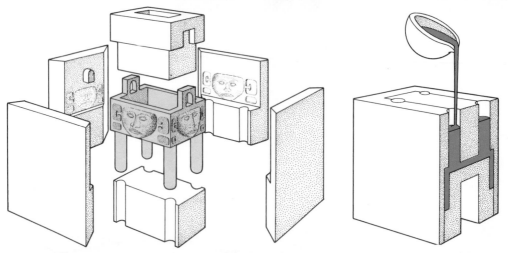

cts and decisions about the calendar which regulated agriculture turned the fate of society.

We know more about some of these things than about the precise way in which early China was governed. The Shang were warriors and conquered their neighbours. They had war chariots and bronze weapons and could put armies of 5,000 men into the field, but their 'empire' (if we can speak of one) was probably a matter of the Shang king demanding and getting tribute and service from local potentates who were otherwise pretty independent. Under the Chou, the dynasty which pushed the Shang aside in about 1050 BC, a still larger area was brought under one ruler, but we know that the way the Chou worked was by leaving government to vassal princes, who ruled over small cities and their surrounding countryside.

One interesting idea which appeared during Chou times was to be very important for later Chinese rulers. This was the idea that the Chou kings – 'Sons of Heaven', as they called themselves – had been divinely appointed to rule; they claimed that they had a 'mandate' from heaven. Though it took a long time, this idea led eventually to the notion that heaven might take away what it had given and withdraw the mandate. When this happened, there would be no obligation to remain loyal to the king. In later times men often justified their changes of allegiance by this idea, transferring their loyalties to new rulers when the authority of the existing kings ebbed away.

Shang rulers were buried in great state. Their tombs have given archaeologists much information about them. One of their practices was to be buried with their horses and slaves – whose skeletons lie round the central pit in this royal tomb from the Shang capital, Anyang.

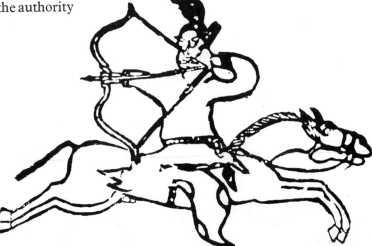

A mounted archer of Chou times; a picture taken from a design stamped on a clay tile.

The discovery of writing

All the civilizations we have looked at so far soon arrived at literacy – that is, some form of writing. Many people have thought that literacy is the essential feature of civilization. Even if not everyone agrees with this, arriving at it is clearly a very important step in a society's development.

We take writing so much for granted that it is worth spending a moment thinking about why it matters so much. In the first place, it makes it possible to keep records. This means that information is much more readily available than it would be among peoples having to rely on traditions handed down by word of mouth. People in non-literate societies often seem to have very good memories; this is because they have to use them to recall much that we would write down. In such societies old people are very important; they are what we would call 'data-banks', storing important information about ways of doing things or arrangements made long ago. But memories are far from reliable. If they are wrong, they cannot easily be checked without written records. An increased capacity for storing useful information is therefore the first great benefit of literacy.

Writing also makes communication much easier: people can send written messages instead of having to go themselves to see someone or having to rely on a messenger's memory. This is a big change, the first step in a speeding-up of communications which has now reached

All over the world many people – like these Tanzanian tribesmen – still rely on stories passed on by word of mouth from generation to generation for their record of what has happened in the past.

a point at which we can speak almost instantaneously to someone on the other side of the world and look at him at the same time.

Finally, the invention of writing made literature possible – that is to say, hearing poems, stories and holy books *read*, instead of *recited* by someone who knew them by heart. Eventually, it made it possible for someone who wished to do so to obtain a copy of a poem or a story, and read it as many times as he liked, when he liked – another fact we take for granted.

For all these reasons, then, the invention of writing was of great importance. As a last point, let us add that it also made the historian's task possible because of the mass of information it made available to him.

So far, so good: writing is a big step in human progress. But what is writing? It is not just sending visual messages; we often do that by making signs to one another, by dressing in certain ways or by carrying out other acts which express meanings, like patting someone on the back. North American Indians sent smoke-signals; English gypsies used to leave pieces of straw knotted or bent in a special way at a house where they had been well received.

Writing is more than just signalling; it is a matter of making signs in such a way as to represent the words of a language. But the distinction can be blurred; even the signs which are made by the signalling flags used by ships are a form of writing, for, if we were to put them down on paper, the different designs of the flags would stand for words and could be read by someone who recognized them.

The signs of this sort which we use most often and are most widely understood are the letters of the alphabet. The origins of the alphabet seem to be in drawing. The earliest languages we know about all seem to have started by using little pictures to stand for the names of things. So many of these were soon needed, though, that such 'pictographs', as they are called, usually changed their appearance and also their meaning. In some languages they came to stand not for things but for parts of words, syllables or sounds. By rearranging them in different orders, many different words could be written with the same signs. In some languages which developed in this way the result was an alphabet of a fairly small number of characters which could be put together in many ways.

Even literate societies still use signs other than words for sending messages. The different symbols for two sorts of cloud on the weather map are one example. Road signs are even more widely understood. They are, for limited purposes, an international language.

The first writing we know of comes from Mesopotamia, where clay tablets with signs scratched on them have been found from as early as 3200 BC. They usually bear little pictures of objects, but we know that even at this date some of the signs stood for numbers and some of the pictures were symbolic – they did not stand for the things they represented, but for words.

Gradually, over the next two or three centuries, these pictures gave way to patterns, each pattern made up of one or more triangular impressions made by a chopped-off reed on soft clay. These patterns came to stand for syllables or sounds and the result was a huge advance in flexibility and simplicity.

This form of writing was called 'cuneiform' and it was enormously successful. The last message known to have been written in it has been dated by scholars to about AD 75, so it had about 3000 years of life – this is several centuries longer than our own alphabet has been in use. The first writings in it were, naturally, in Sumerian (thanks to cuneiform, something like 2000 signs in old Sumerian were reduced to a few hundred), but it was taken up and used for many languages all over the Near East.

No one is quite sure what this carving from Sumer is, though it seems to show someone making some sort of offering. It may be a stone implement and the inscription cannot yet be read in full. But it is one of the oldest pieces of writing on stone yet to be found.

One of the first accountancy documents: a clay tablet of about 2800 BC with lists of fields and crops in an early form of cuneiform writing. It comes from Sumer.

An early mathematics book – a part of a tablet which is a collection of geometrical problems for students in Babylonia in about 1800 BC.

Above: sketches of hieroglyphs ready for carving. They come from the tomb of an Egyptian king of the fourteenth century BC. *Right: wood with inlaid hieroglyphs from about 400* BC. *By then such characters were little used in everyday writing.*
Below: part of a papyrus roll of mathematical tablets and problems written in 'hieratic' with a rush pen. The method may explain why hieroglyph declined. It was hard to draw the figures on a soft surface with a pen.

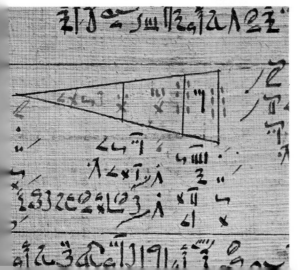

Though they knew about cuneiform, the Egyptians stuck to the form of writing which they had meanwhile arrived at for themselves. This is called 'hieroglyph' and was based on pictographs. (There later came to be a simplified form of it called 'hieratic'.) But they followed a similar path to that of the Sumerians in coming to make the little pictures stand for sounds rather than things. Their signs, though, were much harder to write (and much more interesting to look at) than the Sumerian; hieroglyph never spread as did cuneiform. But it had just as long a life – Egyptian writing was formed about 3000 BC

The Rosetta Stone

In 1798, as part of the war against England, the French government sent an expedition to Egypt under the command of General Bonaparte (who was later to be the emperor Napoleon). A large number of scientists and scholars went with the expedition. Some of them did a great deal of work on the remains of the monuments of ancient Egypt and published valuable accounts of them later. The most important result of their work was the discovery of a basalt slab in a fort near Rosetta, on the western mouth of the Nile. This was to prove the key to the biggest single step forward ever taken in the historical study of ancient Egypt. It had on it inscriptions in three different scripts, Greek, demotic Egyptian and hieroglyph. It at once seemed obvious that they might all say the same thing, but no one could make sense of the hieroglyph until a great French scholar, Champollion, concluded that hieroglyph might consist not of symbols for things, as many had thought, but might have evolved into representations of sounds or letters. He showed that at last the mysterious code of hieroglyph, never before read, could be deciphered. Champollion made this great discovery when he was only 32; unfortunately he died only two years later, though after having made many further contributions to Egyptology and after writing a grammar and a dictionary of ancient Egyptian. By 1851 so much was known about hieroglyph that the names of Queen Victoria and the Prince Consort were both written up in Egyptian characters in the Crystal Palace when the Great Exhibition was held there. The Rosetta Stone, as it is usually known, can now be seen in the British Museum.

The stone (pictured above), which is about 115 cm long and 70 cm wide, has three bands of writing on it: hieroglyph at the top, then demotic Egyptian, then Greek. It was discovered in a damaged condition, with only fourteen lines of hieroglyphs remaining.

and the last known specimen of it was written in AD 394. Because it was so hard to master, though, the secret of reading it was lost for a long time. Scholars have only been able to translate hieroglyph since the beginning of the last century, when writing on the Rosetta Stone was deciphered by a great French scholar, Champollion.

Farther east, the Indus valley peoples used pictographs; these appear on the seals which are the only records we have of the Indus language. Though they cannot yet be fully deciphered, the written language seems to have been fairly advanced, with only a few hundred characters. But it died out, perhaps because of the Aryan invasions. When writing started again in India in about 500 BC, it seems to have been as an imitation of a Semitic alphabet, perhaps brought by merchants. From this were later to come scripts used all over India and in Burma, Siam and Ceylon.

In China, things were very different. As we have seen, Chinese is a very ancient language in the sense that some of its modern written characters were already formed when the first writings – the inscriptions on oracle-bones – appear. These characters (more than 2000 are found in the Shang records) had already undergone a lot of development: they were far more than pictographs by the time the first surviving specimens were written. But Chinese has never evolved a syllabic structure or an alphabet and this has left it a very complicated language. It is in the main true that for every idea there is a different character in Chinese, so that, instead of learning how to spell, the Chinese have to learn to memorize shapes. Even today, to read a simple text needs a knowledge of 2000 or 3000 characters, and writing (done with a brush) is very difficult. Instead of learning an alphabet of twenty or thirty characters and then using them in different arrangements to spell different words, a Chinese child has for several years at school to learn hundreds of new characters each year in order to read his language.

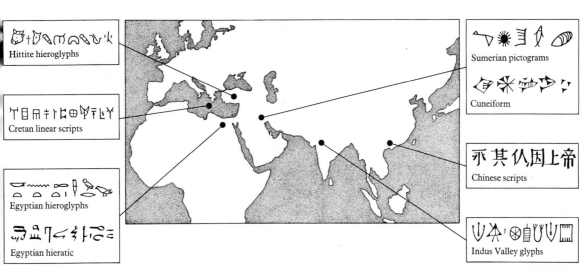

Where some early scripts began.

Writing materials

Cuneiform, hieroglyph and Chinese characters from ancient times survive cut in stone and cast in bronze. Inscriptions in such forms were meant to last, and they did. But such materials could not be 'written' on quickly, nor were they cheap to carry about. Other writing materials were needed if writing was to be widely useful. One such material seems even to have preceded written language itself.

This was the clay tablet, first used in Sumer, drawn on with a stylus or stamped with a seal. Clay was cheap, easily inscribed when wet, but lasting almost indefinitely when baked and properly stored. Tablets of it were easy to carry and so could be used for messages as well as for records. Some were even made with a clay jacket or envelope, so that they could be sealed up and only opened by breaking the covering; this secured them against being tampered with.

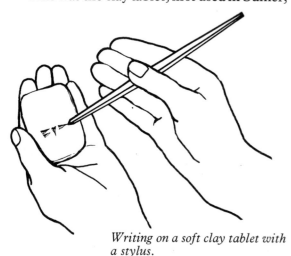

Writing on a soft clay tablet with a stylus.

Above: a contract from Uruk, made in about 1750 BC, and sealed in its envelope by witnesses to guarantee it was authentic. The text of the contract also appears on the envelope, so that it can be consulted without opening.

Left: three ivory writing-boards which had soft wax surfaces, 'leaves' from one of the first 'books', on which an astronomical treatise was written for an Assyrian king in the eighth century BC.

A detail, showing a swallow, from a papyrus Book of the Dead made for a scribe in about 1250 BC.

The papyrus reed, growing taller than a man, and useful for ropes and weaving as well as providing the first 'paper' of sorts.

Imhotep, a great minister and architect of the Old Kingdom, shown with a papyrus roll open on his knee.

Many thousands of clay tablets have survived and, as people have discovered how to read the languages written on them, they have told us a lot about the ancient world. As time passed, though, documents written on another material became more common. This was papyrus, invented in Egypt. It was made from the pith of reeds sliced into strips which were laid side by side. Another layer of strips was then laid crossways on them. The strips were dampened and pounded to make a surface which could be written on with ink when dry. Sheets of papyrus could be joined together in rolls – one which has been found is nearly forty metres long – and these were the first books. Papyrus was a more convenient writing material than clay and was used for more than 3000 years in the Near East.

Though parchment (dried animal skin) also came into use in early times, papyrus was the most common means of writing there until paper (which took its name from papyrus) was brought from China in the Middle Ages. Paper is one of the most important contributions to civilization made by China, but was not invented until somewhere about the first century AD. Before that time the Chinese used silk cloth or bone and wood for their writing.

Scribes

Literacy required a new kind of technician, the writer or scribe. Soon after the appearance of writing in all the old civilizations we begin to find evidence of the existence of scribes. They were often powerful officials, to whom great respect was shown. Rulers depended on them for keeping records and transmitting orders; private people needed their services for writing letters – and for reading them too.

Both Mesopotamian and Egyptian records show the importance of scribes at very early dates. In Mesopotamia the names of some begin to be known from the second millennium. In Egypt there are statues of scribes, some shown with their writing materials; kings themselves prayed that they might serve the gods as scribes. We should not think of scribes just as clerks writing down what other people told them. They rose high in government service and among their tasks was the overseeing of big building operations such as the Egyptian pyramids, or the irrigation works of Sumer.

The first scribes may have been priests, or at least attached in some way to temples. In Europe during the Middle Ages, thousands of years later, few people except monks and priests could write, so that the special connection of writing with religion was kept up for a long time. Nonetheless in the ancient Near East scribes seem soon to have become a group separate from the priests. Theirs was the first of the professions.

For a long time the only schools were schools for scribes. Writing and the sort of mathematics needed for surveying and building were the main subjects to be taught to people who were not priests in Mesopotamia and Egypt. From clay tablets and papyrus which have schoolboys' exercises written on them we know quite a lot about these schools. In Mesopotamia parents paid fees to the headmasters who taught boys Sumerian (which had become the classical language of that civilization even when other languages like Akkadian or Aramaic were used by the peoples who followed Sumer), gave them lists of words to learn, model exercises to write out and corrected their work. A clay tablet has been found which seems to have been crossed out with some irritation, and is full of erasures; perhaps it was an exercise a teacher lost patience with. Another exercise records the story of a pupil who arrived late for school, had a disastrous day and was caned, but who then got his father to invite the headmaster to dinner and give him a new garment. Subsequently, we hear, the pupil is restored to favour and his headmaster prophesies he will have a good future. This is the sort of thing one would expect to find in an exercise book.

In Egypt the profession of scribe became more or less hereditary. Parents who were officials sent their children to school so that they could follow the same career. It is easy to understand why: it must have been much

An Egyptian scribe's palette and pen (made from a rush). The ink was held in the two circular depressions.

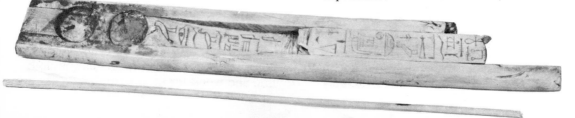

This stone relief from an Assyrian king's palace at Nineveh shows two scribes with different writing materials. One uses a stylus to inscribe cuneiform on a wax-covered tablet, while the other is writing with a pen on a scroll – probably in Aramaic, which could be written in a fairly flowing script.

Egyptian scribes at work: a boy stands ready with a fresh papyrus for them.

more pleasant to oversee the collection of taxes or the conscription of labour for a big building than to work in the fields or in a gang hauling blocks of stone. 'Be a scribe, who is free from forced labour' says one of the sentences Egyptian scholars were given to copy.

Both in Sumerian and Egyptian there was a word for a female scribe, which suggests that women did enter the profession; but this was probably unusual, for there is almost no other evidence of them. Nor is there any sign that girls went to school.

We know nothing about who practised writing in the Indus valley civilizations, but a lot about China, where literacy developed rather differently. There were Chinese scribes, but, at quite an early date, people who were not officials began to write too. The art of writing in the sense of forming characters on the page is called calligraphy, and in China it came to be thought of as one of the supreme skills of an educated man. Just as a man might be admired for his painting or poetry, so he could be admired in China for the beauty of his handwriting. This is understandable when we look at Chinese characters, for it takes great skill to produce them at all. A frequently used character may take a dozen or so strokes of the brush; some take many more. But the total effect is often very beautiful.

Writing and reading Chinese is so difficult that the literate class was cut off from the life of the people for thousands of years. But in all newly literate societies those who can use the new skill form a class quite distinct from those below them. The simpler the forms of writing, though, the quicker its adoption by other classes. The appearance in the first millennium BC of the alphabet we still use was the greatest simplification down to that time and has made it much easier for large numbers of people to read and write. Many countries in this century – Turkey, for example – have rejected other traditional scripts and adopted it.

Languages and literature

Literacy helps to reveal the map of languages used in ancient times. This in turn can sometimes tell us about the often mysterious comings and goings of peoples. For about 2000 years there was a lot of movement in the Near East and elsewhere by people whose languages belonged to a family to which most modern European languages, as well as Persian and Hindi – to take only a few – all belong. These are called Indo-European. Given the Semitic-speakers already there, this left behind a very confused pattern of languages. Later it was to be muddled still more by further arrivals from Central Asia, speaking languages of yet another big group, called Altaic.

It is very easy to lose one's way while trying to follow the detail of such changes. All we need keep in mind here is that, because a common form of writing – cuneiform – was used for many languages in the Near East, it was possible for men to start compiling the first dictionaries of one another's languages at an early date. For a long time Akkadian, the language spoken by the people ruled over by Sargon, and the basis of later Assyrian and Babylonian, was used as a diplomatic language

– that is, for negotiations between rulers – rather as Latin or French was used until recently as the international language of diplomacy in Europe; it was very convenient if everyone used the same language for official business. A big collection of clay tablets forming part of the diplomatic archives of an Egyptian pharaoh of the fifteenth century BC was found which contained documents from all over the Near East, from many different courts and countries, and all were written in Akkadian.

Common languages and ways of writing also made it easier for stories to travel about between peoples. This is what seems to have happened to many tales which have their origins in Sumer. Literature begins there: the oldest piece of literature in the world is called the *Epic of Gilgamesh*, the story of a hero whose name was actually that of a Sumerian king. It was only written down long after its actual composition, but it is the oldest item in a body of old Sumerian literature which was taken for granted as the background of literature in the Near East for thousands of years. Anyone interested in story-telling at all in, say, Babylon

Some cylinder seals from ancient Mesopotamia show scenes from the Epic of Gilgamesh. *This impression (made by rolling one of these seals on wax) seems to show the hero Gilgamesh in a pose he often appears in, fighting a bull. The other figure is also a character from the* Epic, Utnapishtim, *who (like Noah) saved himself from a flood by building an ark. Perhaps this is what the reed boat stands for. Boats are still built in this way on the Tigris.*

1 600 BC would have known who Gilgamesh was and what he did, just as any educated European of the nineteenth century knew about the Greek legend of the siege of Troy. (Sumerian, it is interesting to note, went on being taught to schoolboys in Mesopotamia long after it ceased to be in daily use, just as European children until very recently were usually taught Greek and Latin.)

Early literature helped to pass ideas from one people to another. For example, as the *Epic of Gilgamesh* came down through history, it acquired at some point a new episode, the story of a great flood which wipes out all mankind except for a specially favoured family, who escape from it by building an ark. Then, when the flood goes down, this family re-peoples the earth with its descendants. Now, this story may be very old indeed: floods were frequent in ancient Sumer and the story may have begun with some dim memory of a village trying to put itself to rights and start up again after a familiar disaster. But similar stories turn up in the literature of many Near Eastern peoples – the best known is that of the Hebrew Old Testament involving Noah and his family. We cannot say who learned the story from whom, when this happened, or where; perhaps all early peoples had flood legends. But written literature made it much easier for such stories to travel far beyond the places where they were first formed.

Legends of gods and heroes were not the only subjects of early literature. From the Egyptian New Kingdom there survive much love poetry and some love stories too. Chinese literature begins with a great collection of ballads and poems, the *Book of Songs*. It was not compiled until about 600 BC, but many of the pieces it contains are believed to go back to the early days of the Chou dynasty. The oldest Indian literature, that in Sanskrit, on the other hand, is nearly all religious, with two great exceptions, two epics, probably assembled about 700 BC but not written down for another 1000 years.

These are the *Mahabharata* and the *Ramayana*; the former is the longest poem in the world, about thirty times as long as Milton's *Paradise Lost* and full of stories about gods and heroes as well as of religious poetry.

We owe much to the men who first wrote down these works, but also much to those who first took the trouble to collect them in libraries. One man who deserves special mention is an Assyrian king of the seventh century BC, Ashurbanipal. He was a great conqueror, who liked to show his power in unpleasant ways (he did all he could actually to wipe one of his conquests off the map and on another occasion harnessed the princes he defeated to his chariot), but he deserves to be remembered for a great library of tablets which he ordered his scribes to assemble. Among them were thousands which bore copies of ancient works of literature or inscriptions which have since perished. Of many thousand or so 'literary' clay tablets which survive from ancient Mesopotamia, many come from Ashburbanipal's library at Nineveh. Among them is the final version of the *Epic of Gilgamesh*.

Egyptians often had prepared for their tombs collections of religious texts called the Book of the Dead to help them in the next world. This detail from one dated about 1350 BC shows the sun-god's cat killing the serpent of evil.

Records

Only a minority of the 25,000 or so tablets in Ashurbanipal's collection were in any sense literature. Most of them were administrative and diplomatic records – in modern terms, official papers. This should remind us that people began writing not for artistic but for very practical reasons – the Mesopotamians wanted records of business transactions, recipes, lists of names. Even in China, much later, the characters written on the oracle-bones were there in order to obtain practical answers to important questions – about agricultural prospects, for example. The most important change brought by writing was that it made it possible to store such information.

The Mesopotamians' earliest records – from Sumer – appear to be almost entirely economic, and probably refer to the receipt of goods at temples. The words used show how much economic matters dominated early writing – there are over thirty signs for sheep and goats in early Mesopotamian writing.

Another widespread early use of writing was to set out the chronologies of dynasties and kings. Sooner or later most literate societies did this. The king-list of Sumer is one of the first examples; it tells us how long Sumer's kings reigned, what their relationship was to their predecessors and any interesting incidents of their reigns. It is not very accurate at first (some of the earliest reigns are said to have lasted 1000 years each!) but, as it comes down nearer to 1794 BC (the final date), it improves. Together with inscriptions and dedications left by Mesopotamian kings in temples, it can tell historians a lot from about 2800 BC on-

A stone prism made in about 2000 BC inscribed with a list of the kings of Sumer and Akkad.
Right: an Egyptian record defaced for propaganda reasons – the figure of the queen which appeared in the centre was erased by order of her successor.

wards. The Egyptian and Chinese dynasties were also listed in this way in early records.

Since information is also available from other sources, the value even of single entries in such lists is greatly increased because they can be checked. Later in Mesopotamian history, for example, one list mentions an eclipse of the sun visible at Nineveh. Because we know from other evidence exactly when this occurred – 15 June 763 BC – we can date about two centuries of other entries related to it.

Inscriptions have already been mentioned. Besides appearing in temples, they were also put on victory monuments, or *steles*, in early Mesopotamia. The most famous one has a different purpose, though. This is the black *stele* covered in cuneiform, on which a great ruler of Babylon, Hammurabi I, set up his code of laws, so that all men could consult them and make sure they received justice. This was in about 1790 BC and it can now be seen in the Louvre in Paris. Other kings had done the same before Hammurabi, but his collection of laws is the biggest and most complete to have survived.

Some laws survive from the ancient world only as single commands of a ruler. Others, like the royal decrees of the Hittites, a people who ruled a large part of the Near East for some centuries, have long historical preambles. As we can see from the later records of the Jewish Old Testament, there is also often a lot of non-historical or legendary material mixed up with early legal and official records. Where writing first begins, though, in the Near East and Egypt, the bulk of the material to survive for the first 2000 years or so is economic, administrative and diplomatic record, whether on clay tablets or papyrus and this greatly affects the writing of history. We have a quite different scale of evidence about these times and so real history begins to be possible.

The black stele *inscribed with Hammurabi's code of laws. Hammurabi is shown addressing the sun god Shamash. The* stele *is taller than a man.*

Egyptian craftsmanship and artistry were often very realistic in depicting the lives of individuals. Married couples in affectionate poses and their children appear among the statues, musicians and acrobats are shown entertaining guests at feasts, there are pictures of royal princesses and of a lady making up her face before a mirror. In another, a bereaved family mourns a dead father. Usually made for tombs or for objects to be buried with the dead, such pictures give us a much more vivid picture of the actual life of the ancient Egyptians than we have of the people of any other of the first civilizations.

Mastery over men

Most people now take it for granted that human beings live in big groups ruled by different governments; the usual name for them is 'states'. States are pieces of machinery for doing certain jobs. They have not always existed. They grew out of simple tribal and kinship groups and the first cities. Probably the religious authority of those who controlled or protected the temples was very important in their origins. Early kings were either gods (Egypt), viceroys for gods (Sumer), or like priests in being able to carry out religious ceremonies (China). Almost always they had some sort of religious authority.

By modern standards, early states had quite simple tasks. Yet they were enormously more difficult and advanced than anything that could be done by primitive peoples. The first states not only provided protection, maintained order and imposed laws governing behaviour, as earlier authorities had done, but they upheld service to the gods by organizing the upkeep of temples and big festivals. Above all, they mobilized labour to carry out important collective purposes.

Building and engineering works are the best examples. Some scholars have even suggested that here is one of the main explanations why the state exists at all. Besides the need to find a leader in war or to seek guidance from the priest who could tell them what the gods wanted, the people of ancient Sumer had to be organized in large numbers for digging canals and building dykes if they were to survive at all in their valley. The first government depart-

A Chinese official of late Han times rides out in his carriage. This rubbing taken from a tile shows a favourite theme of Chinese art of this period, which sometimes depicts whole processions of officials and their retainers going on tour.

Most ancient societies were organized in very rigid ranks: people did not move about. At the apex of Egyptian society was the pharaoh, so remote that he was in the end deemed to be a god; below him were officials who directed the peasants on whom the whole structure rested. Only a few specialists – entertainers, doctors, priests – were outside these groups.

ment of which we have any knowledge is the police force of canal inspectors in Sumer, and Mesopotamian law is from the start full of provisions for disputes over water and irrigation. Hammurabi's code, for instance, lays down penalties for someone careless enough to flood his neighbour's plot by mismanagement.

Irrigation mattered less in early Egypt than in Sumer (though some kings recorded their building of canals and dams, and one early title for a local governor was 'canal-digger'), and Chinese records show no interest in irrigation until about 550 BC – so irrigation is not the whole story of the beginning of government. Another part of the story seems to be economic. Some rulers appear to have doled out the produce of the community to specialists after it had been brought to a common centre by a kind of taxation. In early Sumer, for example, it looks as if farmers had to hand over crops (a kind of taxation) to the temples (which in this respect were somewhat like government departments) for them to be handed out again to workers and their families (like wages). The big granaries of the Indus cities may have had this role, too.

A concentration of power is one hallmark of the state. A number of inventions made it much easier to organize men to do things during the first centuries of civilization. One of them was writing. The records we have already spoken of made it much easier to make sensible and consistent decisions and to keep a check on taxes; messages in writing made the delivery of complicated orders and news simpler; communications were easier all round. Information is always a help and rulers could accumulate more of it than other people.

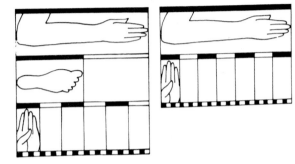

The cubit – the length of the forearm from the elbow to the tip of the middle finger – was the usual way of measuring length in the ancient Near East. The Mesopotamians (left) divided the cubit into two feet, and these into hands and finger-widths; there were six hands to a cubit. The Egyptians (right) had seven hands to a cubit.

An Egyptian surveying-party unwinds the measuring-rope which is used to measure plots of land and so to estimate the crop yields on which taxes must be paid.

Warfare

Another set of changes which made states much more powerful was the development of efficient armies. We are now used to the idea that really devastating weapons likely to have a decisive effect are not to be found in private hands but are monopolized by governments. For most of human history the tendency has been in this direction (though it has to be re-membered that for a long time there was not such a difference as there is today between the kinds of weapons an individual could easily come by and the more powerful ones not avail-able to him). It seems likely that only the rulers who could control supplies of the necessary minerals could have had first bronze and later iron weapons. Their soldiers, armed with these

weapons, and trained and disciplined (there are already pictures from ancient Sumer which show well-ordered ranks of infantry), would have been able to defeat any barbarians, armed only with stone weapons, who could have been persuaded to stand and fight. Even arrows and spears, which both sides might have used, were better if metal-tipped. But, of course, supplies of metals were not always easy to obtain and it was a long time before the rank and file had bronze weapons, which were at first possessed only by the rich. At one time, the Sumerians reverted from using weapons made of bronze (an alloy of copper and tin) to using simply copper again, because their supplies of tin had ceased.

Apart from the coming of iron, the greatest single change in warfare in thousands of years was the use of horses in battle. The art of managing horse and bow or spear at the same time was not easily learnt. It seems likely that such skills were first practised by the barbarian peoples who were for centuries entering the Fertile Crescent from the high-lands to the

Left : model of Egyptian infantry found in a prince's tomb. Right : Egyptian soldiers fighting Nubians from the south. This picture comes from a casket found amongst one of the most famous hoards of treasure ever discovered in Egypt, that from the tomb of the pharaoh Tutankhamon (see page 104).

Gold flies like that shown below seem to have been introduced under the New Kingdom perhaps as a reward for military valour. Later they became purely decorative and were used as necklaces.

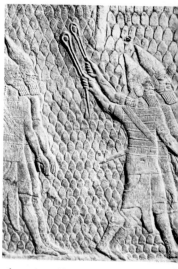

Assyrian slingers. As every reader of the story of David and Goliath remembers, the sling was one of the most powerful missile weapons available in ancient times. Besides suitably rounded stones, lead bullets were sometimes used.

A formation of Sumerian spearmen. Close inspection reveals they are walking over the (presumably dead) bodies of their opponents.

north-east; the place where riding began seems to have been the Iranian plateau. Even these peoples did not have the skills of later cavalry. Though regular armies began to incorporate cavalry regiments from about 1000 BC, it was several centuries before the stirrup was invented which made it possible to charge home.

Long before soldiers took to riding, horses were used to pull chariots (which required the invention of the bridle and bit). The light two-horse chariot with a crew of a driver and another man armed with spear or bow seems to have been used first by a people called the Kassites, in Babylonia, but these new weapons so changed warfare in open country that soon all the great armies of the Near East had chariot arms, much as all armies have tanks today. They spread to India with the Aryans and to China at some later time.

Sometimes such changes had important

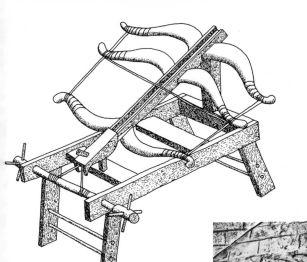

An Assyrian battering-ram in action. The crew are protected by a thick armour, probably of wickerwork and leather.

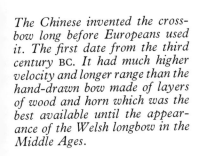

The Chinese invented the cross-bow long before Europeans used it. The first date from the third century BC. *It had much higher velocity and longer range than the hand-drawn bow made of layers of wood and horn which was the best available until the appearance of the Welsh longbow in the Middle Ages.*

effects; some people have attributed the first unification of China, for example, to soldiers with iron swords. At a slightly later date the Chinese empire benefited enormously from its metal-workers' skill in producing the mechanism needed for the cross-bow, a weapon whose bolts outranged the arrows of the barbarians to the north of the Great Wall and which long made safe the empire's frontier on this side.

Fortifications strengthened early states against less civilized peoples, but they also led to the development by ancient armies of special siege-warfare machines. Some of them can be seen on Assyrian reliefs in the British Museum. Their use required specialists and the Assyrian army was an army of technical arms, with slingers, archers, infantry, heavy cavalry and, as it were, artillery. A state which could put a force like this into the field was obviously much stronger than anything hitherto seen.

Sumerian chariots were little more than carts drawn by asses, and were thus unlikely to have been very manoeuvrable.

Managing the unseen

Ancient civilizations did not separate men's thinking into several branches as we now do. Though religion is not easy to define, we think that it is mainly the business of priests and theologians, or of other people who have in some sense a special concern with it. We do not think it is the main business of, say, philosophers, or of scientists, or of mathematicians. Nor do we mix up any of these professions with the practice of magic. Nowadays it is very unusual for educated people even to believe that there is such a thing as magic, and for them 'magicians' are simply people who are very clever at performing tricks which make ordinary things behave in mysterious ways.

Nonetheless for thousands of years people who were educated and lived in the most advanced civilizations thought that things which we separate in this way were really part of one big subject. For a long time the life of the mind

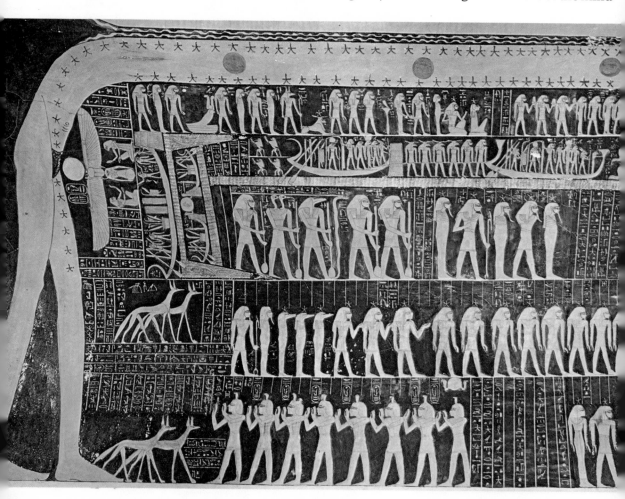

was not something in whose different branches people specialized. Priests, mathematicians, astronomers, magicians, astrologers, doctors were often the same people. Almost everywhere it was believed that powerful gods decided much of what happened in this world.

The Egyptians explained night and day by a myth. They believed that the sky goddess Nut swallowed the sun in the evening and gave birth to it again in the morning. In this picture from the ceiling of the tomb of the pharaoh Ramses VI she is shown arched across the sky, with the sun represented as a red disc at various stages of its progress through her body.

At a very early date priests had appeared who were supposed to be particularly good at knowing what the gods required and at carrying out the necessary ceremonies to please them. Superstitious and silly though many of their ideas now seem, these were the first scientists, philosophers, theologians and mathematicians. Science and philosophy really began with their observations about the way the natural world worked – the movements of the stars, for example – and with their thinking about what they saw.

Most ancient peoples had stories which explained why things were the way they were.

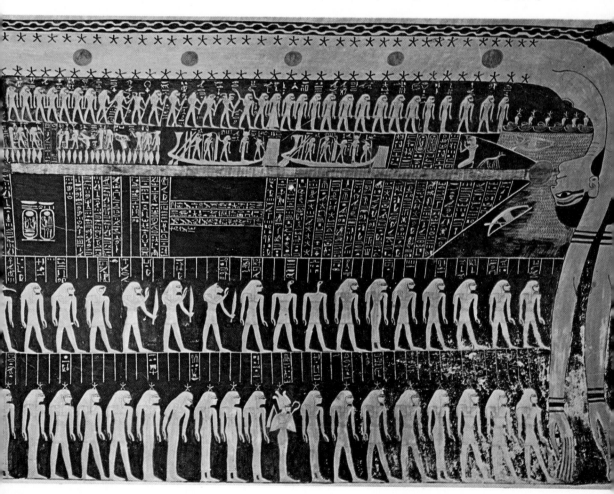

Above: a Sumerian king, pouring out an offering, pays homage to the moon-god. Below: Re, the Egyptian sun-god and supreme judge of the universe, receives an offering.

These are called myths. We know much more about them after the coming of literacy, when they could be written down. There was, of course, an enormous variety of myths, but some show strong similarities to one another. Almost every Middle Eastern people, for instance, has a story about a god who dies or who is carried off, goes down into the earth and is then recovered or reborn.

This probably reflects the need of most agricultural peoples to explain the mysterious 'death' which seems to overtake the land in the winter and then the almost miraculous 'birth' of life again from the earth in spring.

But there could be important contrasts between the myths of different peoples. Very different views were held, for example, by the ancient Sumerians and the ancient Egyptians about the world people would enter after this life. For a Sumerian it was a dismal, shabby place, gloomy and hopeless; the Egyptians thought, on the other hand, that if a man deserved it he might have an even pleasanter version of much the same sort of life he had enjoyed on this earth.

The Labrys, the double axe-head which, with the horns of a bull, is one of the symbols of Cretan religion in Minoan times. It was used as a ritual offering.

Amon-Re was originally a tribal god, but his cult spread from its origin near Thebes until he was worshipped all over Egypt. He took over much of the prestige and mythology of the original Egyptian creation god, *Atum*, whose embodiment was a mud hillock emerging from the primeval watery chaos. Obviously, this reflected the emergence of life each year as the Nile left rich soil exposed when its floods fell again. *Shu* (the air) and *Tefnut* (moisture) were the children of Atum and the parents of Geb and Nut.

Geb, the earth god, and his sister *Nut*, the sky-goddess, were the parents of Seth, Nephthys, Osiris and Isis. The custom of brother–sister marriage, which long persisted in the Egyptian royal houses, is probably reflected in this legend – and, of course, in the story of Horus, child of Osiris and Isis, who were also brother and sister.

Seth and *Osiris* were brothers. The legends about them, which centre around Seth's killing of Osiris (who was resurrected to become in due course king of the underworld and judge of the dead), are a myth of the way in which the original two kingdoms of Upper and Lower Egypt struggled before they were eventually united. According to another part of the myth, this unification was the work of *Horus*, son of Osiris by his sister *Isis*, and the slayer of Seth.

Nephthys was sister of Isis. She helped restore Osiris to life. *Anubis* was the son of Seth and Nephthys. He was the jackal-god of mummification and assisted in the rites by which a dead man was admitted to the underworld.

Such ideas almost certainly go back far beyond the beginnings of civilization. Most ancient peoples had their own gods in whom they had believed since pre-civilized times. These were sometimes personifications of the elements (rain and air, for example), sometimes local and tribal gods, associated with particular places and thought of in superstitious terms as creatures who fought for their peoples against other tribal gods. Sometimes such gods were really not much more than malevolent demons. As the ancient civilizations progressed, though, people began to believe in something subtler and more enlightened. From these ideas came what have been called the higher religions.

Broadly speaking, these placed much more emphasis on the non-material side of religion, on the believer achieving the right state of mind and spirit and on his carrying out his moral duties rather than on his superstitious attempts to placate gods whom he feared. In their highest forms, such developments suggest that even at an early date some people were beginning to have monotheistic ideas – ideas based on the assumption that only one god exists, and that he is the creator and sustainer of all life. For most people, though, even in the centres of the most developed civilization, the religious world long continued to be one of many gods.

A Canaanite god from about 1500 BC. Perhaps this was a representation of the fertility god so often referred to in the Old Testament, Baal.

This idol from early Bronze Age Cyprus (about 2300 BC) is made of terracotta. Vaguely human, it is hard to see what kind of cult it was for but similar works have been found as far away as Portugal.

*An Indian goddess from Mohen-
jodaro. Many such have been
found and it is thought that they
represent a mother goddess who
was the object of a special cult.*

*The 'snake-goddess' of Minoan
Crete was a household goddess, a
friendly figure found in many
shrines. She may have been the
origin of the later Greek goddess
Athena, sometimes portrayed
with a snake.*

66

Mastering things

All societies have toolkits of some sort for dealing with nature and using it for their own purposes. We call them technologies. They developed very rapidly in the early civilizations, but it must be remembered at the outset that this was 'rapidly' only in comparison with anything in earlier times. Technological change in the ancient world was very uneven and very slow for thousands of years. One of the biggest innovations in history, for example, was the replacement of bronze by iron as the main metal in general use, but in many places this happened only long after it happened elsewhere. Although we may speak of 1000 BC as a rough marker of when the Bronze gives way to the Iron Age in the Near East, there must have been many villages where an iron axe or dagger had still not been seen hundreds of years later,

though in big cities people by then took such things for granted.

Technological change at this sort of pace is very different from what we are now used to. Forty years ago penicillin, transistor radios and television by satellite did not exist, yet now they are familiar all round the world. This is something of an illusion, though. Unevenness of development lasted a long time. Even a hundred years ago an iron plough was a rarity in many parts of Russia, and it still is in much of Asia and South America.

Allowing for slowness and unevenness in their impact, though, it is still possible to pick out a number of innovations between about 3500 and 1000 BC which not only enormously increased people's control over nature but also changed their lives in other ways.

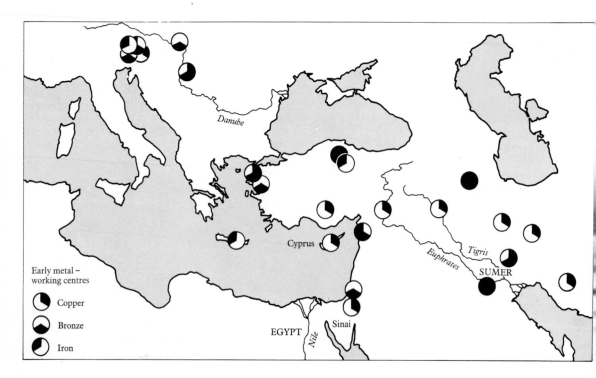

Early metal – working centres

Copper

Bronze

Iron

Danube

Cyprus

EGYPT

Nile

Sinai

Euphrates

Tigris

SUMER

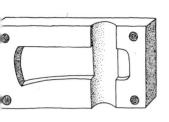

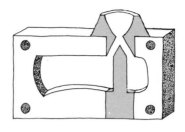

The diagram shows one important step in improving casting techniques – a mould with a removable core to make axe-blades with a socket for the handle to be fitted. Two flat moulds are brought together around the specially shaped core, through the top of which the molten metal is poured. The result is an axe-head like the one shown.

This drawing from a tomb painting shows the process of casting bronze doors. At the top left, a stoker feeds the fire while others use bellows to make it blaze up. Below, a crucible of molten metal is lifted from the fire. In the centre, the bronze is poured into a mould. Materials are brought in from the right, while above is a representation of a finished pair of doors.

Metallurgy

A knowledge of gold, silver and copper goes back into prehistory. The first metal-workers of Sumer and Egypt inherited techniques of hammering these metals to shape and for a long time this was the way that most precious metals were processed. Then someone discovered how to cast copper by pouring it into moulds. Next came bronze (though it may have been known earlier in Thailand). In another 1000 years bronze became widespread in the Near East. A few hundred years later the Chinese were casting it too. It was the most important metal in use for most of the period discussed in this book.

The coming of bronze made a great difference. An alloy of copper and tin, it was expensive but easier to cast and harder than copper alone. It was therefore better for tools and weapons. Bronze seems to have been used pretty generally for tools in Egypt after about 2500 BC. Metal-workers knew how to cast copper long before 3000 BC – again, we do not know how they discovered the process – but the lower melting-point of bronze meant that they could turn out a better-quality product. Important improvements in the process of casting followed as time went by. Bellows driven by the feet were in use for furnaces in

Egypt not long after 2000 BC. A few hundred years more and the quality of the alloy had been improved by the addition of lead, which made better casting possible, and a technique had been found for making hollow objects in moulds.

Iron only began to replace bronze in the Near East in about 1000 BC, though 500 years later it was known in all the great centres of civilization. For a long time no one except the Chinese, whose knowledge was not shared, knew how to cast it. Iron had to be forged – that is, heated and then hammered into shape.

Where this method first began is still no known, but it seems that it was the Hittite who first had iron in any quantity. Also the eventually discovered how to temper stee The coming of both bronze and iron mean that mineral-bearing areas became much mor important. We hear about Egyptian minin expeditions, accompanied by soldiers, to th Sinai desert for copper; and Cyprus, rich i copper, begins to figure prominently in trade It has been suggested that the empire of Sargo I of Akkad (see page 18) is really to be explaine by his wish to control sources of minerals.

A tomb-painting showing Egyptian gilders and goldsmiths at work.

Left: Hittite arrow-head and sickle made of iron. Right: gold jewellery of about 1500 BC from Crete. Two bees holding a ball of honey form a buckle or clamp.

Tools and manufacturing

Metal tools made a great difference to crafts-manship. The first builders of pyramids had only tools of copper or harder stones to shape the limestone blocks they used, and bronze made their task much easier. As for smaller-scale work, such as carpentry or boat-building, an even greater change was made by the arrival of iron. The actual design of tools, on the other hand, does not seem to have altered very much during these years. For the whole of this period bow-drills were virtually the only means of drilling.

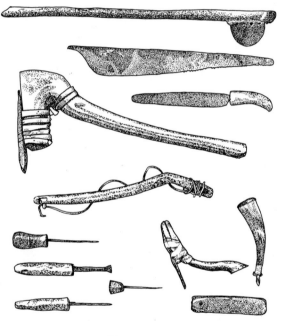

Egyptian carpentry and joinery was of a very high standard, though produced only with tools edged with beaten copper such as those shown on the left, which date from about 1500 BC. The carpenter's vice did not exist, so timber was lashed to a firm upright for sawing (as above), with a saw set to cut on the pull rather than (like modern saws) on the push. The only drill available was a bow-drill, shown in use at the right below. The two men working on the table next to the driller are smoothing it with sandstone. Having no planes, the Egyptian could only smooth to a rough finish with adzes and then had to finish work in this way.

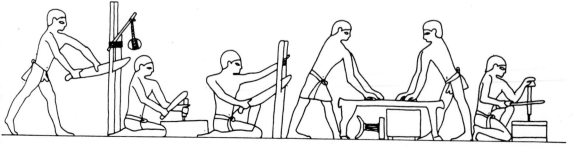

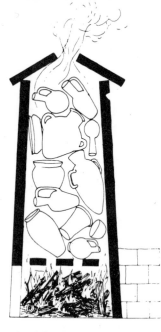

Potters used a wheel, but not the one we know – one driven by the foot or some other means, so as to leave both the potter's hands free – until about 700 BC; before that, it was more like a turntable, turned by one hand.

Weaving changed in one important respect in the Near East in that horizontal looms were replaced by vertical ones which took up less floor-space and could be used indoors more easily. This affected the process of manufacture, though the way the cloth was made hardly changed in principle. There were no important innovations in machines for handling materials, either, and certainly nothing comparable to those devised in warfare.

Egyptian potters at work with a hand-turned wheel. A diagram (above) showing the inside of the kiln is also given. No kilns have in fact survived.

An Egyptian loom of about 2000 BC. Though it appears to be upright, it is in fact one which lies flat.

Left: a Mesopotamian lady of about 800 BC holds a distaff with which she is spinning some kind of thread.

Agriculture

The coming of iron was one of the major technical innovations in agriculture. Bronze axes could be used for attacking trees, but iron would turn heavier soils. This, however, was not the only reason why agricultural output increased: improvements in irrigation and the plough were also crucial. The introduction of the sharduf in Mesopotamia, in about 2000 BC, provided the basic means of small-scale irrigation in the Near East from that day until now. With its help a man can lift 2700 litres of water a day.

The plough mattered even more, though. In the earliest picture that we have (from a Sumerian seal) it is shown drawn by humans; another of the Sumerian 'firsts' was their harnessing of animals to it. Until about 2000 BC

This picture from about 1250 BC shows a gardener using the sharduf *which is still widely used today for irrigation of individual plots of land.*

Egyptian plough

Sumerian seed-drill

Cretan plough

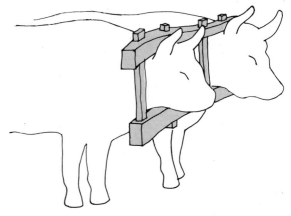

Early yokes greatly increased the pulling power of oxen, but the ploughs behind them could still scrape only very shallow furrows. The Egyptian plough shown here is the oldest and simplest kind, still rather like a forked branch with a draught-pole lashed to it. The Sumerian plough is more advanced and has a seed-drill attached, and the Cretan version is single-handed.

oxen pulled the plough with their horns, an inefficient as well as a cruel method, but then came another important change: the invention of the shoulder-yoke. Finally, also in Mesopotamia, the shape of the plough changed and it became a machine to turn the soil as well as scratch a furrow in it. The result was an instrument whose efficiency had been enormously increased in 2000 years or so and it was soon put to another use, when a seed drill was added to it.

Rural Egypt. Right: a peasant assists at the birth of a calf on this relief. Below: cattle are driven past their owner during a census. These models were placed in the tomb of a Theban nobleman in about 2000 BC so that he should have the use of his wealth after death.

Changes in transport

For hundreds of thousands of years it was very difficult to move about the earth's surface except on foot. This meant that there was very little exchange of ideas and institutions between different communities living only a few kilometres from one another. Some of the most important changes in technology during the period of the first civilizations, therefore, were those affecting transport.

On land, once animals had been domesticated, this was really a matter of finding better ways to use their muscle-power. One simple way was to make the animal itself carry a load, evolving harness and saddling arrangements to make this easier. Much early traffic in goods was by pack-horse, or donkeys and asses. In some arid zones the camel became very important as a transport animal after its domestication in about 1500 BC. Even bigger advances followed from the improvement of the wheel, and the development of better yokes and harness for draught-animals. There were solid-wheeled carts in Sumer in about 3000 BC, but, though these are still used in some parts of the world, they were much more cumbersome than the carts with spoked wheels which evolved from them. Horses were certainly drawing carts of this sort in about 2000 BC in north-eastern Iran.

Early carts were not likely to stand up well to long journeys over rough tracks. Chariots had first copper and then iron hoops put round their wheels, but for a very long time such metals were too expensive for ordinary carts. This was one reason why, in places where it could be used, water was so much better a means of transport, especially for bulky goods over long distances.

For a long time the Egyptians did not adopt the wheel for transport, preferring to use sledges even for fairly light loads – in this case, a body for burial.

Right : the Egyptians learnt the value of the chariot from their enemies. This example, drawn by mules, seems to have a peaceful purpose with a canopy to protect the driver from the sun.

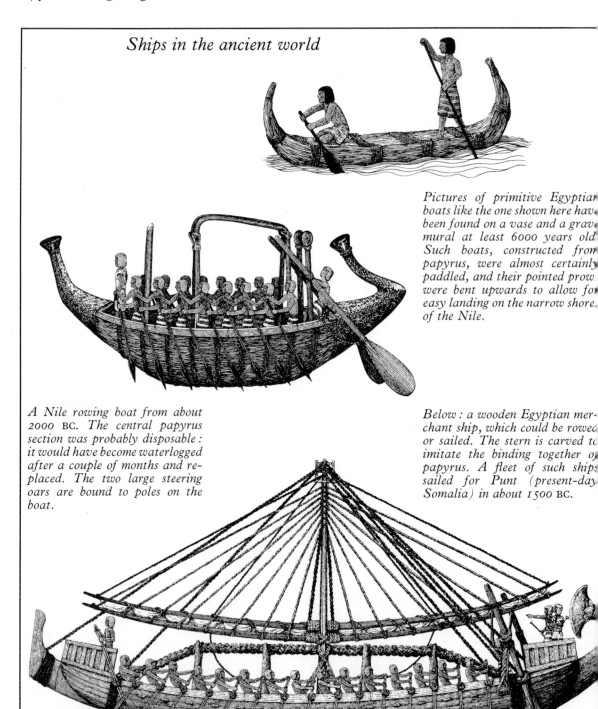

Ships in the ancient world

Pictures of primitive Egyptian boats like the one shown here have been found on a vase and a grave mural at least 6000 years old. Such boats, constructed from papyrus, were almost certainly paddled, and their pointed prows were bent upwards to allow for easy landing on the narrow shores of the Nile.

A Nile rowing boat from about 2000 BC. The central papyrus section was probably disposable: it would have become waterlogged after a couple of months and replaced. The two large steering oars are bound to poles on the boat.

Below: a wooden Egyptian merchant ship, which could be rowed or sailed. The stern is carved to imitate the binding together of papyrus. A fleet of such ships sailed for Punt (present-day Somalia) in about 1500 BC.

Understandably the islanders of Crete were great sea-farers. This small sailing-boat dates from about 2000 BC.

Left: an eighth-century Phoenician warship. Each side of the boat held two lines of oarsmen sitting on different levels; the men on the upper level are hidden in this picture. A narrow fighting deck ran down the centre, allowing the soldiers to move around without upsetting the balance of the boat.

An example of a magnificent Minoan vessel, from a fresco at Thera. The prow and stern are decorated with leaping dolphins, and the ship is paddled rather than rowed.

Early commerce

We take commerce – buying and selling things – for granted, but know very little about how it started. For many centuries before civilization had existed people were exchanging goods and services and even using something like money to help them do so. But when they actually began to do this and how, we do not know.

This is partly because it is difficult to know how to interpret early records of goods being moved about. Some of these transactions were probably tribute, or gifts, and it is not easy to separate such things from trade. An example (in reverse) may make this clearer; people usually give tips to taxi-drivers because it is the custom of our society to do so. Yet such tips used only to be given when the person to whom they were given had actually done some extra service over and above what was expected. It would be very difficult, though, to say exactly when the change took place.

It is hard even to be sure what went on in local markets in ancient times. We know, for example, that Egyptian peasants used to bring their produce to village-centres and that they took away in exchange things other people had brought, but whether these were markets in our sense, where relative values are fixed by bargaining, is hard to say.

We do know that it was a long time before money was invented. Money makes complicated trade possible yet, even before it came into existence, there were units of account in which what was due for the upkeep of Egyptian workmen was reckoned and in which different kinds of goods could be valued against one another. The actual exchange of counters for goods or services – money – only came much later, though. It may have grown out of the existence of ceremonial objects – knives, bars or ingots of metal, bronze vessels – which were given by monarchs to one another as presents and about whose approximate value there was

Two early examples of currency. Left: the man on the bronze stand (which comes from Cyprus) is carrying an ingot of metal – possibly iron – shaped like an animal hide. Right: a piece of bronze money, in the form of a hoe, from China of the fifth century BC. *Many early Chinese coins were shaped like implements.*

Tribute to a pharaoh. Syrians bring gifts, including a little girl, probably a slave, to the Egyptian ruler in about 1400 BC.

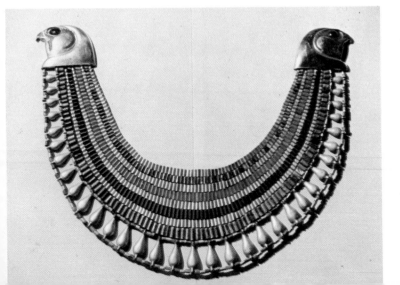

A collar – made in this case for a dead wearer, since it was placed in a tomb – of gold foil, faïence, turquoises and carnelians.

general agreement. The first coins were not made until about 700 BC.

Another thing which commerce needs if it is to operate effectively is some system of accepted weights and measures. By about 2000 BC Egypt, Mesopotamia and the Indus valley cities had all achieved this.

When trade did begin to get under way, it rapidly began to link places and peoples very far apart. Some peoples were especially well placed; the Cretans and the early civilized peoples of mainland Greece both did a lot of trading, possibly because sea-communications were easy in the Aegean. Bahrain, too, was a commercial centre to which traders came from India and perhaps farther east, as well as from Mesopotamia and Egypt. The greatest of the trading peoples, though, were the Phoenicians who lived in a cluster of cities on the Levant coast and enjoyed a golden age of commercial prosperity from about 1000 to 700 BC.

Trade made some parts of the world important because they were the sources of rare materials wanted elsewhere. The Phoenicians seem to have been supplying Egypt with cedar wood well before 1000 BC and the Bible later records the fame of the cedars of Lebanon. The Phoenicians also became famous for their dyes; they made a special purple from the shell-fish found off their coasts.

Standard weights in ancient Mesopotamia were often carved – we do not know why – in the form of a duck preening itself.

From a huge palace at Khorsabad comes this relief showing Phoenicians loading timber in their ships. They handled a big export trade in cedar from the Lebanon, as readers of the Bible will know.

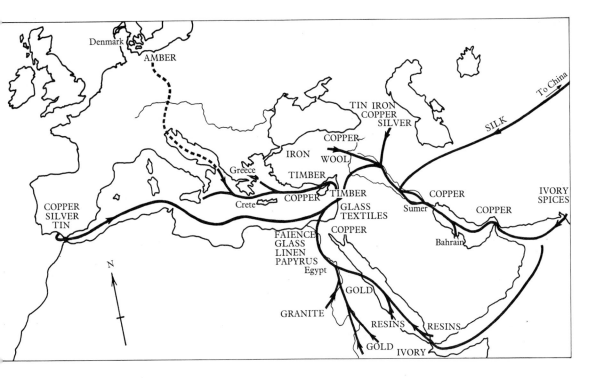

Some routes by which raw materials came to the Near East.

Some sources of such materials were very far from the places where the customers were to be found for them. Thus amber was brought from the Baltic coast to the Aegean, and iron from central Europe to the Near East. Silk came from China to Mesopotamia. Spices came up the Red Sea from the Far East to Egypt; the Egyptians, during a period of a thousand years or so, exported a particular kind of jewellery, faience, over all the world then known to its inhabitants. Horses were bought in Trans-Oxania for the Chinese emperors.

At a very early date the Chinese discovered how to obtain silk and make from it the beautiful materials which came to be all the more prized elsewhere because for so long their origin was mysterious. This rubbing from a stone relief of Han times shows the spinning of silk thread.

The great migrations

Similarities between different civilizations show how rapidly they began to learn from one another. Their interplay became more and more frequent as time passed and it will be useful to consider for a moment why this was so. A rough overall view of what was happening from about 2000 to 1000 BC provides a helpful chronological background.

The first thing to notice is that, during this thousand years, China's history moves at its own pace – it has almost no connection with the rest of the globe. As we have seen, it was in this age that Chinese civilizations began, but the ups and down of Chinese history have virtually nothing to do with what is happening elsewhere.

This is not quite so true of India. The Indus cities were certainly in touch with Mesopo-

tamia. Moreover the great change in India history around about 2000 BC was very close related to events farther west. This change wa the coming of the peoples whose languages a Indo-European or Aryan. If we look at th events of the next thousand years in Ira Mesopotamia, the Levant, Egypt, the Aegea and even in Europe, they all show the impa of Indo-European migrations from the nort These movements had begun long before th period, but they became much more obviou after about 2000 BC.

The Indo-Europeans seem to have con originally from southern Russia. What s them moving is very hard to say. The be guess is that climatic changes, possibly i Central Asia, drove other peoples to the ea of them to migrate towards them, and th

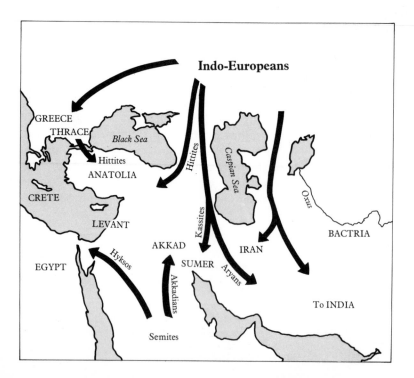

Right: Kurdish refugees i modern Iraq. Their plight is pe haps not very different from the of many displaced peoples in th migrations which shaped th ancient Near East. But the de tails of those migrations will prob ably always be unknown to u The map, for instance, is not in tended to be anything but a sug gestion about the general directic the nomads of the ancient worl might have followed.

ed to pressure on them to move too. The up-shot was that some of the Indo-European peoples pressed into the Balkan peninsula and down to what is now Greece, and from there or from Thrace across into Anatolia; others moved into Bactria, on the banks of the Oxus, and from there moved later into Iran (which is actually the same word as 'Aryan'), and then into India.

These were nomadic peoples, driving herds of cattle and sheep, though they were later often to settle and take up agriculture. They seem to have been horsemen at an early date, and they brought with them into the Near East and India the two-wheeled chariot. Their religion stressed sacrifices to gods who lived in the sky and the importance of fire.

As they entered the Fertile Crescent, these peoples came into conflict with the Semitic peoples who had dominated it since old Sumer was overcome by the Akkadians. But, of course, the Semitic peoples were moving about too. The legendary story of the Jewish people began in Ur, from which Abraham is described in the Old Testament wandering across Meso-potamia and the Levant looking for pasture. This is probably a folk-memory of the history of one of the many tribes who were on the move at this time. Such Semitic peoples met the Egyptian empire when they reached what is now Sinai and Palestine.

In the Near East Mesopotamia was the most attractive area to the outsiders. Invaders experienced and then spread the advanced culture they found there even more widely. As a result a large area of the world came to share much that had originally been the sole posses-sion of the city-states of Sumer – and, almost incidentally, made it possible for this legacy to be in due course passed down to us.

It is worth recalling this confused back-ground of folk-migrations whenever we look at the history of one of the old centres of civilizations in these centuries. It can too easily be made to seem much neater and more clear-cut than it was. Almost certainly, millions of people who then lived and died can have had very little grasp of what was really going on as invaders came and went about them, but the result was an enormous mixture of cultures.

Mesopotamia after Sumer

Movements of peoples had deeply affected the history of Mesopotamia well before the fall of Ur. As neighbouring peoples learnt new skills and ways from the civilizations of the river-valley, Mesopotamia more and more resembled a crucible into which one new element after another was introduced to be mixed up with what was already there.

Among the Semitic peoples pressing into the area from the south were the Amorites. After the fall of Ur, there was a series of little Amorite kingdoms stretching from old Sumer across to Syria. Among them one tribe was especially important because it was able to set up another state, centred in Babylon, in southern Mesopotamia, a Semitic empire like that of Sargon of Akkad nearly seven centuries earlier. From this time Babylon was to be the symbolic centre of the Semitic peoples of southern Mesopotamia, the site of the temple of the greatest god, Marduk.

This empire is still remembered chiefly fo the reputation of its greatest ruler, Han murabi. He ruled a wide tract of territory, bu is more famous for his code. It tells us a grea deal about Babylonian society in nearly 30 articles drawn from earlier judgements an rules covering a wide range of topics – land law, doctors' fees, wages, and divorce amon them. Perhaps it is even more interesting fo the evidence it provides of the solidity an regularity which governments had by the achieved. The point of the code, after all, wa that the same law should be applied by th king to all his subjects.

The first Babylonian empire outlaste Hammurabi, who probably died in about 175 BC, but its kings began to lose their norther

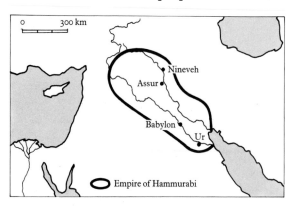

A Babylonian catalogue of stars from before 1000 BC. To the Babylonians we owe not only some of the earliest accurate astronomical observations, but also names of constellations we still use.

The Hittite war-chariot. This relief shows the way the chariot was used, as a platform for an archer or spearman who was free to use his weapons because the driving was left to a second man.

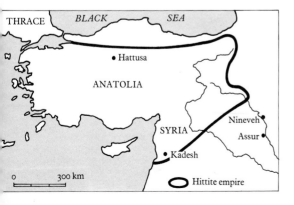

lands in the next century. In about 1600 BC came disaster: a people from the north struck in the valley, plundered and ravaged Babylon, and that was the end of the second Semitic empire in Mesopotamia. Yet it left behind a lasting reputation for the splendour of Babylonian civilization and the skill of its wise men. Babylonian astrologers made important observations of the stars and developed the Sumerian mathematical legacy.

The invaders from the north were an Indo-European people, called Hittites. Until the beginning of this century all that most people knew about them was that they were mentioned many times in the Bible. Even scholars knew little more than that a few items in Egyptian and Mesopotamian records referred to a Hittite empire. Archaeologists only began to excavate Hattusa, the former Hittite capital in Anatolia (in modern Turkey), in 1906, and what they found almost at once – 10,000 or so cuneiform tablets – quickly revealed that this was an important people, who for hundreds of years helped to shape the history of western Asia. But it is only very recently – since 1950 or so – that deciphering the Hittite language has made much progress.

As it looks at present, the Hittites came to Anatolia from Thrace in about 2200 BC. They slowly consolidated their position, and their kings added to their lands until, in about 1700 BC, they ruled a big arc of territory from Syria to the Black Sea. From this they went on to their triumph over Babylon – the high-water mark of the first Hittite 'empire'. There seems to have followed some centuries of internal division and external disaster, an eclipse of Hittite power. Then, after 1400 BC, the Hittites began to conquer again; they had an advantage in possessing iron weapons. This time they finished up ruling lands from the Levant to the Persian Gulf. A Hittite princess married one of the pharaohs. But in the end they too went under to another wave of invaders from the west, the Phrygians.

Assyria

When the Hittites went back north after destroying the first Babylonian empire, a long period of confusion followed in Mesopotamia. One thing which stands out in the confusion, though, is that from this time southern Mesopotamia, centred on Babylon, tended to follow a separate course from its northern neighbours. There emerged in the north a state called Assyria, whose centres were the cities of Nineveh and Assur, high up the Tigris. This had not been a part of the valley where agriculture had been easy enough for civilization to develop of its own accord. The Assyrians were a raw frontier people in origin, learning their civilized ways from farther down the valley.

To judge by the stone reliefs and pictures they left behind from a later age, when they were top dogs in the Near East, the Assyrians were not very agreeable neighbours. They seem to have been cruel, aggressive and domineering. But perhaps they had been forced to be so in order to survive, because the history of Assyria for most of the second millennium BC is of invasion and counter-invasion by one after another of her powerful neighbours. Besides the Hittites, there were the Hurrians (a Caucasian people) and the Mitanni (Indo-Europeans). The Assyrians had something of a breathing-space at the very end of this period; after the Hittites had collapsed, one Assyrian king briefly conquered Syria and Babylonia. But this did not last, because some Semitic tribes called Aramaeans soon took much of this from them.

So many names reflect the confused picture we have of what was happening from about 1300 to 900 BC. But afterwards, down to 646 BC, when the Assyrians' power seemed to be at its height, the story is clearer. Here we have to jump ahead somewhat: in 646 the Assyrians made their last important conquest and completed an empire which at its greatest extent included the whole of Mesopotamia, much of the highlands to the east, Syria, the Levant and Palestine, and even Lower Egypt. This was the biggest united state the area had yet seen.

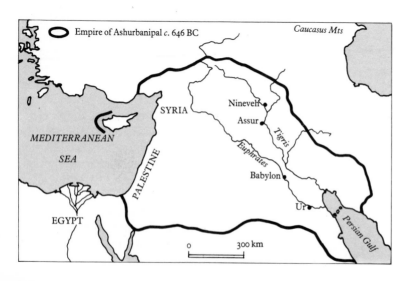

Opposite : a stone relief of Ashurbanipal, the last great king of Assyria. His time was not wholly spent in fighting and hunting — he built up a great library at Nineveh.

A scene from the stone reliefs of Ashburnasirpal's palace at Nimrud; a city is attacked by Assyrian forces while swimmers, some supported by inflated animal skins, try to reach safety within its walls.

A reconstruction of the appearance of Sargon II's great palace at Khorsabad, occupied only for his own reign.

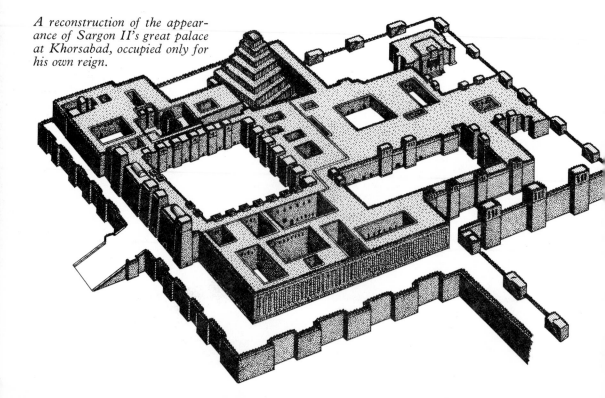

It made a great difference to the life of the Near East, because the Assyrians ruled the area as a unity as earlier rulers had not done. There were revolts and troubled times, but it was a remarkably successful structure of government while it lasted. Instead of simply taking homage and tribute from subordinate kings and princes, the Assyrians in many provinces swept them away, replacing them by Assyrian governors reporting directly to the king in Nineveh. The whole area had the same system of government and law, and one language – Aramaic – was widely used throughout the empire.

Even the harsh side of Assyrian government – and it was very harsh – helped somewhat to mix up the peoples of the Near East, for they were conscripted as soldiers or, if unlucky, deported as slave labour. Even whole populations were moved.

This empire paid for a court of splendour. One great king built a palace at Khorsabad, near Nineveh, on a site which covered over a square kilometre of land, though he hardly lived there before abandoning it. It was decorated with almost one and a half kilometres of the stone reliefs which were the main form of Assyrian art. In their reliefs and in monumental architecture the Assyrian kings expressed their sense of their supreme power – gods do not often appear on Assyrian reliefs, unlike those of Egypt, unless to approve the deeds of kings. Conquest, hunting and receiving tribute and submission are the main themes of the stone carvings, but this is not quite the whole story of Assyrian kingship. It was Ashurbanipal (668–26) who collected the records and literature of ancient Mesopotamia.

One of the first and most sensational excavations of the nineteenth-century archaeologist Sir Henry Layard was the palace at Nineveh of the ferocious ninth-century Assyrian king, Ashurnasirpal. Among his discoveries were a number of colossal half-bull, half-man figures placed at the doors of the palace.

The origins of the Jews

In Egyptian inscriptions of about 1400 BC appears a new word, *apiru*, meaning, it seems, a 'wanderer'. This is the first appearance of the word we translate as 'Hebrew'. The people to whom this name was applied were to produce a greater impact on world history than even Egypt itself, because of the ideas and inspiration which stemmed from their culture. Yet their original resources were tiny, in so far as we know about them at all.

The Hebrews believed themselves to be descendants of Abraham, a patriarch who was said to have led his people from Ur to Syria and Canaan (as the ancients called Palestine). Later, the family of Jacob, Abraham's grandson, is said to have established itself in Egypt (this branch was later called 'Israel'). All this may well be true, though we have only the evidence of the Jewish traditional history set out in the first five books of the Old Testament (the 'Pentateuch') at a much later date to support it. But there were many such Semitic-

A copy of an Egyptian wall-painting showing a Semitic tribe with their herds asking permission to enter Egypt.

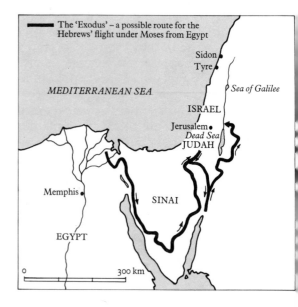

language migrants in the middle of the second millennium BC, and there are no good grounds for denying the story or its outline.

Whatever we choose to believe of the events recorded in the Pentateuch (which did not take the form it now has until shortly before 600 BC), one fact which stands out clearly is that in the thousand or so years before this the Hebrews somehow underwent a religious revolution. It ended with their arriving at the first enduring religion which was 'monotheist' – that is, based on a belief in only one god. They came to believe that their particular tribal god, Yahweh, had promised that, in return for their allegiance to him alone among gods, he would bring the Israelites back to Canaan, the 'promised land', to which he had once brought Abraham out of Ur. This was a very important idea, though a simple one. The Israelites were told that if they *did* something, then something desirable *would* follow.

Giving service to Yahweh alone by worship and obeying his law gradually led the Israelites to despise other gods as inferior. There was also an important difference between Yahweh and other gods – no images were to be made of him. Later came the ideas that his power and presence were not confined to any place but were universal, that he ruled all men, whom he had created, with the same laws of morality. Finally came the idea that no other god existed but him. This was a fully developed monotheism and it took a very long time to reach this point. But it was of immense importance because – again, to look a long way ahead – out of this tradition were to come both Christianity and Islam, religions which have had a worldwide impact.

Meanwhile the Israelites somehow arrived in Canaan from Egypt at about the beginning of the twelfth century BC. The Bible tells us that their great leader was Moses (interestingly, an Egyptian name), who also was the first great law-giver of Israel, though the Commandments associated with his name cannot be dated to a time when he could have been alive and are probably much later.

The Israelites had to fight both the iron-using Philistines and other Semitic peoples in order to establish themselves in Canaan and they also quarrelled among themselves. But there was the tie of common religion to hold them together against outsiders, and soon (perhaps about 1000 BC) they had kings, of whom the first, says the Bible, was Saul. Israel was hardening into something more like a state. Perhaps they profited from the temporary eclipse of greater powers. Solomon, fifty years or so after Saul, was a king of Israel with real international standing, who had an army with a chariot arm and allied with the Phoenicians. He built a magnificent temple in the nation's capital, Jerusalem, which became the focus of the cult of Yahweh.

Soon religious leaders called the Prophets began to attack moral laxity and social injustice. This is another landmark in the history of the Israelites. The Prophets were not just soothsayers and wise men such as could be found in many Near Eastern countries. They were preachers, poets, political and moral critics who claimed that God spoke through them. They were believed and revered by the people. The Prophets invented the bad conscience, so to speak, and brought to its height the Israelite idea of a universal god, just and merciful to those who repented of their wicked ways and turned to him for help.

After Solomon's death in 935 BC, Israel fell on bad times. The kingdom split into a northern half, Israel, and a southern, Judah, which was centred on Jerusalem. The Assyrians obliterated Israel in 722 BC and carried off its peoples into slavery. Judah hung on until 587 BC, when a Babylonian army destroyed the temple and carried the Judaean survivors off to exile. From this time it is possible to speak of the 'Jews', the nation defined by the religion passed down from the ancient Hebrews through Israel and Judah.

Ancient Crete

We should now go back somewhat in time and consider other civilizations outside the Near East. One important centre was the island of Crete, on the south side of the Aegean sea.

By about 2500 BC there were already well-laid-out Cretan towns and villages built of stone. They seem to have been the work of inhabitants drawn in part from peoples who had been there a long time and in part from more recent immigrants from Asia Minor who brought with them Bronze Age skills. Then, in about 2000 BC, the Cretans began to build a series of magnificent palaces. The greatest of them was at Knossos. When they were first excavated in the last century, it was obvious at once that they were the work of a very highly developed civilization indeed.

Scholars have called it 'Minoan', a name taken from the legend of a king Minos whom the Greeks believed to have been a great king in Crete. But there is no other evidence that he ever existed. This civilization prospered for five or six centuries, probably because it did well out of a growing trade with Greece and other parts of the Aegean, Egypt and the Levant. Some Cretans went to Sicily and even, perhaps, traded far up into the Adriatic. Those who stayed at home grew large quantities of olives for oil and grapes for wine and raised many sheep.

They were seafarers too, confident enough of the protection their ships gave them to build towns and palaces without fortifications. The palaces show the Minoans liked comfort. They had elaborate bathrooms and piped drains, but also magnificent decoration. Cretan

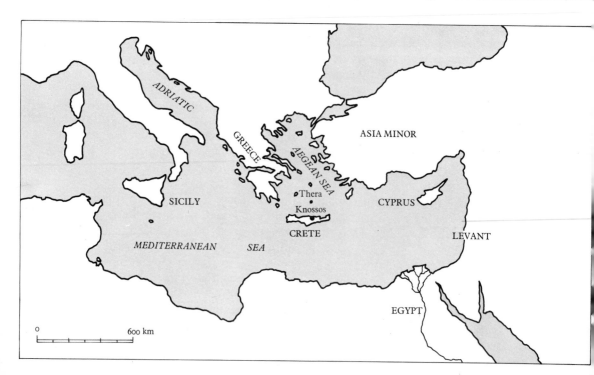

art was to influence Egypt and Greece and has left us some beautiful frescoes from which we can guess a little of the appearance of the ladies of the court at Knossos, of the Cretans' mysterious sport or cult of bull-leaping, and of the flowers and plants of the countryside and the fish of the sea round the islands.

We do not know much about how Crete was governed, but a large collection of administrative tablets found at Knossos suggests it was centralized and very concerned with regulating the economy. Much decipherment still remains to be done. But one interesting and important fact has emerged: while some of the earlier tablets are written in unknown languages, later ones, dating from about 1450 BC, are written in Greek. They are our earliest evidence of the use of this language.

This fits what seems the most likely sequence of events after Minoan civilization declined after 1500 BC. The towns and great palaces were then destroyed, probably by a large earthquake or an eruption elsewhere in the Aegean. Knossos, like other parts of the island, was afterwards occupied by people from the mainland and seems to have prospered again. These people were presumably Greek-speakers who took over Cretan ways of administration. Then, about 1400 BC, Knossos was destroyed by fire. It was never rebuilt and it was the end of civilized Crete for nearly a thousand years. It was always to be remembered as a legendary place of wealth and riches by later peoples in the Aegean.

A tablet from Crete with characters written on it in a script which scholars call 'Linear B' – the first in which we have words written in Greek.

Bull-leaping. A fresco (much restored) from Knossos shows how this mysterious sport – or ritual act – was carried out. Bulls seem to have fascinated the ancient Cretans. Later Greeks addressed the god Poseidon (god of the sea and 'earth-shaker') as a bull and it may have been that the bull was a symbol of the forces of the earthquakes common in the Aegean.

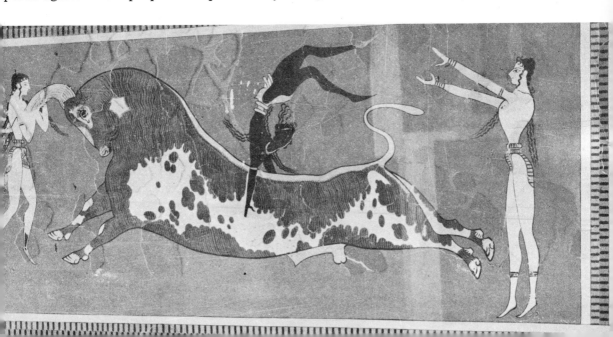

Knossos. *Near the modern town of Heraklion on the northern coast of Crete stood the greatest palace (right) of Minoan times, Knossos, the centre of a pretty large town. Excavating its huge complex of buildings took over thirty years – the restored courtyard around the staircase is shown below right. The palace was lived in for about five hundred years before the great eruption or earthquake on the island of Thera of around 1500 BC, and was then occupied by invaders from Greece. They lived in it for some hundred years or so until it was finally destroyed in a great fire. When this happened is much debated among scholars. This was the end of centuries of Cretan civilization and the palace was not repaired or rebuilt.*

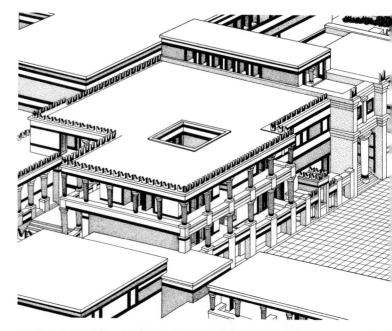

Mallia. *Fifteen miles from Knossos another great palace of Minoan times was built at Mallia. This huge storage jar was found there.*

Thera. *Thera or Santorini is the most southern of the Cyclades islands and the nearest to Crete. Frescoes from the palace there portraying people and animals are shown here, as well as a collapsed staircase. A volcanic eruption took place at Thera in about 1500 BC. It was without parallel in ancient historical times and may have caused the first destruction of Knossos.*

Mycenae

The Greek-speakers who came to Crete and lived at Knossos in its last century or so came from the mainland, and probably from the peninsula we now call Greece, but their ancestors had not been there for very long. They had come from further north, perhaps around 2000 BC, when the people then living in the peninsula, though not very advanced in their ways, were already in touch with Asia. The Aegean is not a big sea and, although it can be very stormy in winter, the hundreds of little towns on its islands and on the mainland of Asia Minor and Europe were able to reach one another much more easily than a similar number of communities inland, because communication by water was much easier and faster than over the same distance by land. As the example of Crete suggests, contact with the mature civilizations of the Near East and Egypt was very stimulating. So, for the people who came to live in Greece, was that with Crete.

The picture of the way civilization developed in Greece and the Aegean is much blurred by the comings and goings between different centres. But perhaps we shall not be far from the truth if we think of two different and opposing currents operating for about a thousand years – people were pressing down into Greece and Thessaly and then crossing the sea to settle islands and towns in Asia Minor, while knowledge, skills, ideas and inspiration were all the time coming the other way from the older centres of civilization.

The first invaders who entered Greece in about 1700 BC were barbarians by comparison with the Cretans, but, like some other barbarian peoples, who came later, they knew how to ride horses and they had chariots. They built strongholds – they seem to have been very wary about dropping their guard, which may tell us something about the way they treated

A Mycenaean bowl found in Cyprus. It dates from about 1300 BC, when the Mycenaeans' overseas trade was flourishing (some scholars think they have found traces of it even in the British Isles).

the natives – some of which were on sites later to become famous as Greek cities. Athens was one. Their most important centre was at Mycenae, and this has given to these people and their culture the adjective we use of them – Mycenaean.

The Mycenaeans were impressive builders and great warriors. They seem to have lived in a sort of league or federation of settlements each ruled by a king, with the one at Mycenae having some sort of presidency or primacy over the others. The aboriginal inhabitants of Greece became the tenants, serfs or slaves of the landowners, the Mycenaean nobles.

By about 1400 BC, when the Mycenaeans had occupied Knossos, their civilization and military ascendancy was at its height. They were active traders too, who were treated with respect by the Hittite kings. Their colonies in Asia Minor prospered. Tablets from about 1200 BC found at Pylos show that they were learning about more advanced techniques of government from their neighbours.

Then, suddenly, darkness sets in. How the end of the Mycenaean supremacy came, we do not know, but it looks as if it may have been touched off by some sort of dynastic quarrels in mainland Greece. At about the same time the whole eastern Mediterranean was in upheaval; raiders whom the Egyptian records call 'Sea Peoples' were harrying the Egyptians under the later kings of the New Kingdom and there may have been Mycenaeans among them. Some scholars have thought the event on which the later Greek story of the siege of Troy was founded was a big raid from mainland Greece on the cities of Asia Minor in about 1200 BC. But we do not know much about such details. By about 1000 BC, though, the first civilization in Greece had been overwhelmed. One cause was the flooding into the peninsula of yet more invaders from the north.

About them the evidence is fragmentary, but it seems likely that (as later legend suggested) these peoples determined the shape of

The 'Lion Gate' to the citadel at Mycenae was probably built in about 1250 BC and is the oldest surviving piece of monumental sculpture in mainland Europe. With their heads (now destroyed) the lions must have been much bigger than a man. What they represent is not known: perhaps they were some kind of badge or coat-of-arms, perhaps guardians.

Mycenaean warriors shown on a vase. The little objects attached to their spears are probably bags containing each man's rations.

Once believed to be the funeral mask and portrait of Agammemnon, the leader of the Achaean expedition to Troy portrayed in Homer's Iliad, this is now thought to be that of a Mycenaean king or prince of about 1500 BC, who was buried with other notables inside the citadel at Mycenae.

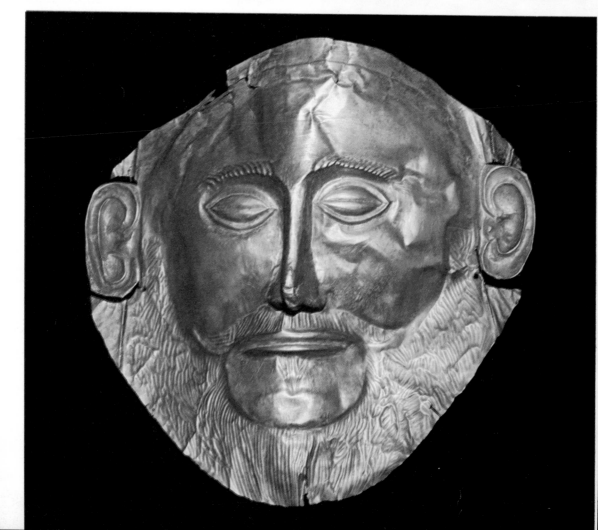

Clay idols from Mycenae, perhaps images of gods who were later to pass into Greek mythology.

Mycenae: a view showing the citadel standing up above the walls of the town.

future Greece by the settlement of their tribes. One group, speakers of a dialect called Doric, founded communities at what would become Sparta and Argos and then spread out to Crete and the southern coasts of Asia Minor. Another group, the Ionians, settled Attica (the land round Athens) and spread into the Cyclades and the Asian coast, later called Ionia. There were others whose distribution was dictated by the way the valleys ran on the mainland and the siting of convenient harbours on the coast and islands. However it happened, what these settlers were doing was laying out the ground-plan of a future Greece whose peoples were long proud to speak the dialects which showed the original divisions of these invaders.

Archaeologists are still uncovering more about these invaders. A little of their life is reflected also in the two long poems which are the beginning of Greek literature, the *Iliad* and the *Odyssey*. Like other ancient writings, they were not written down until centuries after they were put together, so we have to be careful in using them as evidence, but they suggest a society of barbaric warlords, certainly not as civilized as the Mycenaeans nor with such advanced methods of government. Yet they were the human stock from which the greatest civilization of ancient times was to stem.

The land of the pharaohs

Not much is exactly known about how the Old Kingdom of Egypt declined, but its government seems to have grown weaker, and some people have thought that in the end it more or less fell apart, with local bigwigs running their small areas very much as they liked amid revolts and upheavals. There are signs that there were foreign invasions too. What is at least certain is that, from about 2300 BC, Egypt was going downhill. One symptom, repeated at later bad times in Egypt's history, was that the royal tombs in the pyramids were broken into and looted.

In the next thousand years or so, strong kings twice pulled things together. The second time this happened was the beginning of what is called 'the New Kingdom', when ancient Egypt was not only at the height of its power, but produced some of the most beautiful art to survive from the ancient world.

At its greatest extent the empire ruled by the kings of the New Kingdom included Nubia to the south (which meant much of the modern Sudan) and Palestine and Syria to the northeast. One king even led an army across the Euphrates. Egypt was a great power; its army had chariots (though they seem to have been adopted only after a successful foreign invader had used them to seize the delta). It was under the New Kingdom that the kings of Egypt were first called 'pharaoh', the name used for them in the Bible. The word had originally meant only 'king's home' or 'palace'.

The pharaohs, like earlier kings, were great builders, though they did not build pyramids like their predecessors. One reason for this was that pyramids tempted robbers, and so royal tombs began to be built in rocky hillsides in lonely places. The 'Valley of the Kings' is the greatest of these sites. The buildings of the New Kingdom are mainly temples, of which

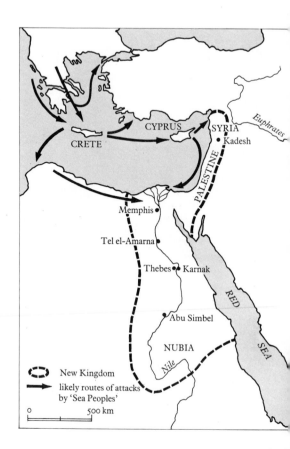

Karnak and Abu Simbel are among the most striking. Like the pyramids, they were built of stone; the dwellings of most people were still built of mud-bricks which have crumbled away. Even big and important centres like Memphis and Thebes have left little trace. One pharaoh of the New Kingdom, though, planned a new town at Tel el-Amarna as a royal residence and centre of government. It was later sacked, but excavations there have told us a lot about what an important Egyptian centre was like. The temples and government offices, of course, were built of stone, but private homes were sometimes plastered and

Left : the temple at Karnak, near Thebes, was originally built in 2000 BC for the sun-god Amon-Re but successive pharaohs added to it greatly as the centuries went by.

1. A diagram of the great hall at Giza (built about 2500 BC). The only features allowing light to enter are the narrow chutes (A). 2. The hall at Karnak, built over 1000 years later, has taller and more graceful pillars, as well as larger openings for light (B).

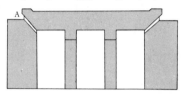

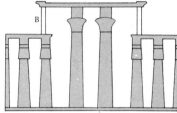

Below : another great temple to Amon-Re was built at Luxor, only a few kilometres from Karnak.

painted. The houses of rich people often had stone thresholds, lintels or window-frames and had large gardens opening off one of the main streets; the hovels of the poor were squeezed in higgledy-piggledy wherever there was space. There was no drainage at all; rubbish seems to have been thrown into any convenient hole in the ground. Tel el-Amarna (or Akhetaten, as the city was then named) must have been a smelly place, once away from the enormous palace or the enclosure about a kilometre long by 300 metres broad in which was built the great temple which dominated the town.

This temple was the real reason why the town was there. During the Old Kingdom an official religion had been established. It found room for many variations of belief and local cults and was the religion of Egypt until the reign of the king who built Tel el-Amarna. He seems to have tried to break with the past by imposing a new and monotheistic cult on Egypt. The temple was dedicated to the god Aton, whose symbol was the sun. This is one of the first examples of monotheism we know about, and no doubt it irritated the priests of the old temples, who must have had vested interests in the old order. This may explain why the pharaoh – who changed his own name to Akhnaton ('he whom Aton loves') – decided to move his government away from Thebes, where the old religion was well established, and build his new capital.

Whatever his motives, Akhnaton's reign was marked by big efforts to make the new religion prevail (he sent people round to obliterate the names of older gods from royal tombs and monuments, for example). Yet, when he died, the new religion collapsed.

Akhnaton, the pharaoh who tried to introduce a new cult, shown worshipping the sun, its symbol.

The magnificent tomb of a woman pharaoh, Hatshepsut (1503–1482 BC). Carvings and statues in the temple glorify the Queen and describe one of the most famous events of her reign – an expedition by Egyptian traders to Punt (present-day Somalia).

Ramses II (1290–24 BC) was one of the most successful of Egypt's rulers, and he built for himself two unique cliff temples at Abu Simbel, high up the Nile in Nubia. Left: four huge statues of Ramses II overlook the Nile. Right: the interior of the temple.

Akhnaton's successor was a young man who also changed his name – but to one which showed he respected the old gods: Tutankhamon (Amon was the name of an older deity). He died young and does not seem to have been a very impressive ruler, yet his name is perhaps better known than that of any other pharaoh. This is because, when his tomb was found about fifty years ago, it contained a more magnificent collection of beautiful and precious objects which had been buried with him than any other royal tomb (most of which had long ago been broken into and robbed).

The sight that greeted the excavators of Tutankhamon's tomb when they finally penetrated eight metres of rubble to enter the first chamber, piled with the pharaoh's possessions.

Besides beautiful objects, the New Kingdom also produced literature, men of learning and some able astronomers. The Egyptians had already devised a calendar based on the solar year – they were the first people to divide the year into $365\frac{1}{4}$ days. They also had a great reputation for medical knowledge.

Not many Egyptians would have known much about such things, nor would they have seen much of the beautiful art of the New Kingdom. Most of them were peasants, their way of life (of which we can see something in many tomb-paintings) hardly changing for thousands of years. They were governed by civil servants who kept their side of affairs running in a remarkably unchanging way too. In the end this may be why the New Kingdom fell on evil days. From about 1200 BC there were attacks from the outside by 'Sea Peoples' (they may have come from the Aegean or the Levant), while there were signs of trouble within Egypt. By 1000 BC the kingdom was divided by rival dynasties. Though there were occasional flickers of recovery still to come, Egypt's great days were over. Perhaps it was just because her traditions went back so far that her rulers found it hard to deal with a world which was beginning to change rapidly. But a continuous history of civilization for 2000 years was an impressive performance to look back on.

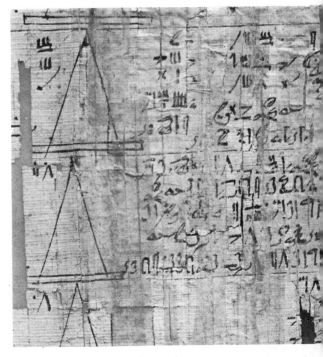

How to measure a pyramid. Part of a mathematical treatise.

Toys belonging to Egyptian children.

Tutankhamon owes his fame not to anything he did – he was a pretty unremarkable ruler – but to the men who built him a tomb secure enough to defeat the efforts of tomb-robbers. Among the hundreds of things it contained were the solid gold mummy-case of the pharaoh himself, his throne, on the back of which is a picture of him attended by his queen, papyrus sandals, a relief showing the pharaoh hunting, and jewellery ornamented with a beetle or scarab – a very common form of decorative symbol.

The fringe of the old world of civilization

As we have seen, civilized societies existed by about 1000 BC in three large, distinct areas of the world: the Near East, India and China. For all its internal troubles, the Near East, together with Egypt and the Aegean, made up an area where civilization was so solidly established and had already changed life so much that it is difficult to see how any permanent setback into barbarism could possibly have occurred. This was already the 'old world' of civilization.

Civilization exercises an effect on its neighbours. On the one hand, ideas and influence spread outwards from it; on the other, it attracts attention and investigation – sometimes of a rather brutal kind – from those who envy its wealth and accomplishments. Further afield still, its needs for scarce resources can affect other areas not in direct contact with it. In these respects, India and China were perhaps somewhat more insulated and cut off (though never completely) than was the old-world zone.

To the south, Egyptian civilization helped to provoke the appearance up the Nile at Napata of an independent kingdom called Kush. Its people were probably not dissimilar in stock to the Ethiopians. They had arrived at a hieroglyphic writing (which has not yet been deciphered) and so were the first Africans to achieve literacy after the Egyptians had done so.

Their hieroglyphics may have been learnt from Egypt. Certainly the Kushites learnt so much from that source that they became strong enough to conquer Egypt itself in 730 BC; Kushite kings thus provided the twenty-fifth dynasty of the pharaohs. They were overthrown in their turn by the Assyrians, and retired again to the south. The Kushites then began to direct their attention the other way and to expand into the Sudan. They thus carried civilization further into Africa. Kush became a more negroid kingdom, and also acquired important mineral resources, in particular deposits of iron ore. The Kushites had learnt from the Assyrians how to smelt iron, and their capital of Meroe soon became something of an African Sheffield or Essen, an outstanding metallurgical centre. From Meroe the knowledge of iron-working began to be diffused to the rest of Africa, over which it took a thousand years or more to spread.

With the exception of Kush, Africa remained pretty much untouched by early civilization. This is understandable: there were huge barriers of distance, terrain and climate in the way once the Sahara had begun to dry up (a process which began in prehistoric times). For some reason there appears to have been less stimulus for change here than elsewhere. Consequently Africa had to wait for thousands of years before it was brought within the ambit of influence of other civilizations and acquired such devices and skills as the wheel, literacy and intensive agriculture. Like metallurgy and the higher religions, all these came to Africa from outside.

To the west of the old world the trading peoples of Mycenae and Phoenicia had carried the seeds of civilization a long way. The latter were, in due course, to found a scatter of settlements all round the western Mediterranean and even outside it, for the Spanish port of Cadiz was founded as a Phoenician settlement.

Europe north of the Mediterranean coasts and Greece was a different story, visited by occasional traders from the Near East, but still a barbaric and in many respects backward region until shortly before the Christian era. Yet it was not unimportant to more advanced societies. Though the peoples of northern and

The Phoenicians ran a very successful trade in coloured glass, which they exported all over the Mediterranean.

Ruins of a Phoenician temple at Byblos in the Lebanon, the city whose name the Greeks took as a word for a book.

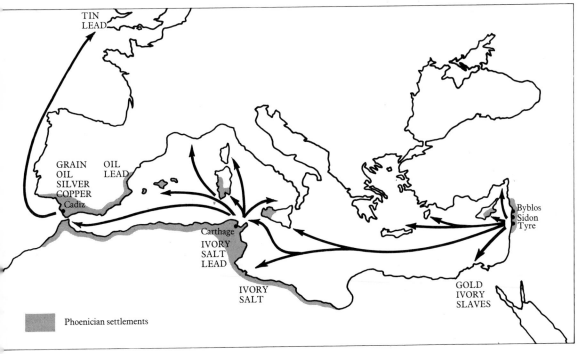

TIN
LEAD

GRAIN   OIL
OIL   LEAD
SILVER
COPPER
Cadiz

Byblos
Sidon
Tyre

Carthage
IVORY
SALT
LEAD

IVORY
SALT

GOLD
IVORY
SLAVES

Phoenician settlements

western Europe, like the Africans, had to wait for literacy to reach them from the old centres of civilization, they were outstanding metal-workers and some of them were remarkable builders.

It now seems that copper was being worked in the Balkans in about 5000 BC – nearly 2000 years before civilization appeared in Sumer. Europe's minerals and skills were eagerly sought by prospectors and traders from the Near East from 3000 BC onwards, and a thousand years later there were important metal-working centres in Spain and Italy, as well as in the Balkans. Of course, by modern standards,

One extraordinary example of what could be done by the skilled smiths and metal-workers of prehistoric Europe – a bronze ceremonial cart, presumably used to carry some offering or sacrifice at a ritual ceremony, found in a grave at Strettweg in Austria. I dates from somewhere between 800 and 600 BC.

only tiny quantities were involved. Nonetheless the metal-workers of Europe made important positive contributions to human progress.

Who were the European peoples? The answer is very complicated, because migration was going on for thousands of years. A rough guide to Europe in about 2000 BC, though would show the original inhabitants (sometimes called 'West Mediterraneans') for the most part pushed down into Spain and western France. In the middle of the continent and spilling across to the British Isles were an Indo-European people who had pushed them out, the Celts. In the east, on the upper Dniester, were the ancestors of the later Slavs, and in the north, in Scandinavia, Teutonic tribes. Even farther north were the primitive Finns, whose descendants still speak one of the few European languages which does not have an Indo-European base.

Most of these peoples were backward if we compare them with the cities of Assyria and Babylon (though perhaps the contrast would not be very great if we looked instead at the life of the agricultural villages of Anatolia or the Ganges valley). But they had to their credit one very impressive achievement which has caused much excited speculation. This was the building of great stone monuments, or 'megaliths' (a word derived from Greek words meaning 'big stone').

Nothing comparable with these is to be found in the steppe-lands of eastern Europe and south Russia, where no material for them existed and the slow movements of peoples are even harder to trace. Further east still, the beginnings can be detected of further folk-movements which were to alter the destiny of the Fertile Crescent. Much later the Greeks had legends of centaurs, creatures half-men, half-horses, and it is just possible that the origins of the legend lie in dim memories of horsemen from the steppes who were so skilled – in archery, as well as in riding – that horse and rider seemed to be one animal. From the eighth century BC one people of such horsemen, the Scythians, were pressing down the Black Sea coast towards Europe and from the Caucasus into Iran. This was the first entry to the area by the Central Asian peoples whose onslaughts were to make up much of its history in the next 2000 years.

A horseman from the steppes of Russia. This Scythian felt wall-hanging, now preserved in a Leningrad museum, dates from the fourth or fifth century BC.

Aryan India

Whether or not the 'Aryan' peoples (the name usually given to the Indo-European invaders of India) actually destroyed the settlements and cities of the Indus valley, they gradually spread across northern India until by 1000 BC they were to be found over most of the upper valley of the Ganges. They did not wipe out the peoples who already lived there, but settled beside them and dominated them.

When they arrived in India, they were probably in many ways less civilized than the peoples of the Indus cities. Equipped with bronze weapons and chariots, they were originally nomads and herders, but seem to have settled down to farming and to have established villages and cities. Because they built in wood, though, archaeologists cannot tell us much about them. Nor did they leave written records: writing did not reappear in India until about 500 BC.

Nevertheless the Aryans left much more of a mark on later Indian history than did their predecessors; the foundation of much that is still there today can be traced to them. Their written language, Sanskrit, is the basis of Indian languages still spoken, and their religion shaped Hinduism, the religion which is still that of the majority of Indians. Another striking feature of later Indian life, the organization of society into castes, is also Aryan in origin. Castes are groups of people who share the same occupation and who alone are entitled to follow it. The members of a caste, ideally, marry only with one another, have special ritual practices and observances and, if strict, will eat only food prepared by others of their own caste.

There eventually came to be hundreds of castes and sub-castes, but this all began with the simple Aryan division of society into three classes: the Brahmans (or priests), the warriors and the farmers. These groups were not at first so closely defined nor so exclusive as they later became. Soon, though, a fourth class of people seems to have been singled out; this contained the original native population, darker-skinned than the invaders, who wanted to keep separate from these natives, and therefore regarded them as outside the three-class system altogether. These were the 'unclean' who, because they were not Aryans, could not take part in religious sacrifices. In the end they became the so-called 'untouchables' of modern India, a class to which was left the dirty work of scavenging and cleaning: they were so looked down upon that some Brahmans even thought that their shadows falling across food would pollute it.

Since Aryan India left behind neither much archaeology nor written records, it may well be asked how we come to know about it. The answer is through literature, one passed down for centuries by word of mouth. The most important early work of this literature is called the *Rig-Veda*, a collection of a thousand or so hymns put together somewhere about 1000 BC. It gives a clear picture of Aryan religion – one of sacrifice to sky gods – but also much data about Aryan society. Like much early literature (the *Epic of Gilgamesh*, for instance), it was not written down for a long time – not until more than 2000 years later, in fact, in about AD 1300 – but great importance had been attached to its exact memorization, so that we can be fairly certain that it did not change much in being passed on.

The Vedic hymns give us a picture of an India in which the Sanskrit-speaking Aryans and a dark-skinned native people lived side by side in farming villages in the upper Ganges valley (southern India developed much more slowly and was not penetrated by Aryans in the same way). Later in the country's history,

.rchaeology adds to this picture. Iron made its .ppearance in India in about 1000 BC and, as .lsewhere, a big difference to agriculture followed. More important still for food supplies was the fact that by 500 BC the Indians had begun to cultivate rice, a skill they may have learnt from Burma or south-east Asia. It made possible a big growth of population in the Ganges valley, which, because of this, was always to be the focus of Indian history.

Writing began again in India in about the .ixth century BC, when coinage also made its appearance. Northern India was at that time divided into somewhere between a dozen and twenty separate states, some of them kingdoms ruled by local dynasties, some of them (particularly those in the foothills of the north) apparently more like republics. In one of these Gautama was born in 560 BC.

He was to become one of the greatest religious teachers of all time, best known by the name he later acquired – the Buddha, or 'enlightened one'. Gautama worked out his religious teaching in trying to solve his own problems. He was a nobleman or prince, who as a young man might have expected a comfortable, well-off, agreeable life, but who rejected this. He wanted, instead, to discover a way of life which would enable him to understand the true and lasting reality which he believed lay behind the continual changes of human existence. He started from the traditional religion of the Brahmans, but soon went beyond this, finding their emphasis on rituals and sacrifice superficial. In the end he began to teach a way of disciplining mind and body, freeing them from human passions, lusts and fears so that the soul might achieve what was called 'Nirvana' – a state of union with the final reality or godliness which he thought lay beyond life, and one of complete fulfilment and peace. He also taught the importance of good conduct. In this way, he thought, men would be able to break out of the endless cycle of being born again which was the pattern of existence taught by the religion of his day and by later Hinduism.

Gautama travelled a great deal and had great success as a teacher. It is by no means clear, though, that what became known as Buddhism, the religion developed by his followers from his teaching, really expressed his views. His own teaching required no temples or priesthood. Nonetheless it had great success, eventually spreading over all Asia. In this sense Gautama was the first founder of a world religion.

There are many statues and pictures of the Buddha, but none are from his own time. This one depicts him fasting – this is why he is so thin – in order to discipline the body and achieve spiritual enlightenment.

The first Chinese empires

When the Chinese came to look back on their early history, they often wanted to emphasize its natural evolution towards a single government for all China. Because of this, they tended to underrate the importance of times such as that of the later Chou dynasty, or what was called (significantly) the 'Warring States' period – the centuries from about 800 to 221 BC. Yet in these 600 years many things happened which greatly affected China's development. These years were no more barren of achievements in culture, technology and art than were the centuries of upheaval in the Near East and Aegean around 1000 BC.

For one thing, there was more to eat than in former times, mainly because of two developments: iron implements and bigger and better irrigation and flood-control works. Both made it easier to cultivate more land. What followed was that the Chinese population became bigger and China became (as it has remained) the most populous country in the world.

This increase in wealth also gave rise to much more trade. One sign is that copper coins gradually came into use; by the third century

Part of the Great Wall of China.

Believing that jade helped to preserve the body after death, a prince of Han times had this suit made for his wife's body, and another for himself, from over 2000 pieces of jade wired together.

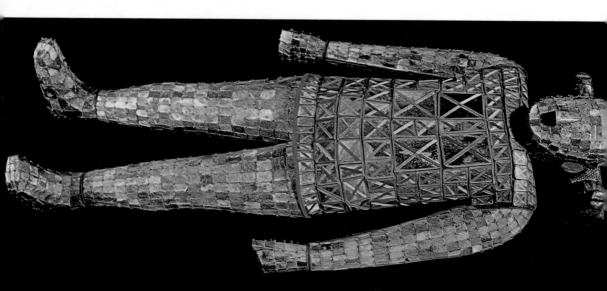

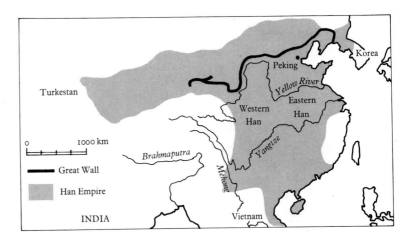

The Han empire at its greatest extent.

BC copper 'cash' was the usual currency, a copper coin with a small square hole in the middle so that it could be put on a string with other coins. It was still in use until a century or so ago.

Governments, as elsewhere, became stronger. They were able to put bigger armies into the field and to equip them with iron weapons. Soldiers mounted on horses (cavalry) appeared, replacing the older chariot forces, and the crossbow was invented. Some rulers began to build long walls to protect parts of their states from the northern barbarians: these were later to be connected up and become the famous Great Wall of China.

Chinese culture gradually spread southwards during this period and by 500 BC Chinese kingdoms already included most of the Yangtze valley. Though there were about ten different states at this time, one eventually emerged which was able to dominate all the others and set up the first unified Chinese state. This was ruled by a dynasty called the Ch'in (after which China is in fact named) and, though later empires often lost control of parts of this territory, the idea has remained that the whole of China is the proper area for a Chinese government to control, whatever practical independence China's regions and local divisions might enjoy. In fact, for most of Chinese

history, central government cannot have been very noticeable to the majority of Chinese.

China has natural frontiers but, under the emperors of the Han dynasty, which followed the Ch'in and ruled (with one interruption) from 202 BC to AD 220, Chinese power went far beyond them. In the north-east it reached into Korea, in the north as far as the Ordos mountains and in the west it conquered Turkestan. One Han general seems even to have reached the Persian Gulf. China began to export silk to Europe and was known in the west, even if only by hearsay, as a great and powerful empire with a high civilization.

By then this civilization already showed many features which would last until the twentieth century. One of the most striking and important of them was a very remarkable civil service. In some ways it was one of the best the world has ever seen, at least in terms of orderly and regular administration. This was in the main the creation of the Han emperors. There had been educated administrators in earlier times, but now they were organized in a regular civil service with an examination system for entry to it. Below the level of the imperial family and the great court nobles, China was ruled for 2000 years by administrators chosen solely for their talent.

Preparing for the examinations was a long

A tile rubbing, showing peasants threshing.

and difficult business; training was expensive in time and money. Not surprisingly therefore most Chinese civil servants came from landed families who could afford special coaching and study. Nonetheless the competition was real, and this meant not only that very able people ran the administration but that they were likely to be independent of outside influences. They looked only to the emperor for orders. This greatly strengthened the state, which no longer needed to rely on local potentates.

For centuries the subjects of the civil service examination were classical Chinese historical and philosophical writings. Among them special attention was given to writing attributed to the greatest of Chinese teachers, Confucius.

He was born in about 551 BC into a minor family of the nobility. As a young man Confucius worked as an administrator for a prince but then withdrew from active life and began to meditate upon questions of right and wrong. Gradually his teaching became famous. In outline, Confucius taught that men's lives should be ruled by the principle of order; there was a proper place for everything, he thought, in the well-run family or in the healthy state, and doing good consisted in finding your proper place in that order and respecting the places of other people and things in it.

This was not the sort of teaching which looked favourably on change – let alone revolution – and, when the ideas of Confucius came to be taken up later as the official philosophy of the empire, they tended to reinforce existing ways of doing things. As civil servants were trained to think in this way, the state became tremendously stable, at the cost of the rejection of new ideas. Chinese administration was very reliable, but also conservative and easily shocked by novelties.

Nonetheless Chinese government did great things. The Great Wall, which separated cultivable China from the regions occupied by nomadic peoples who from time to time attacked China, was completed by the first Ch'in emperor. It is more than 2200 kilometres long. At the same time great works of irrigation and flood-control were carried out in the Yellow River valley. The campaigns mounted far afield by the Han also show the strength of a great state. Finally, there was the big task of regular government: it looks as if under the Han something like fifty million people may have been ruled from Loyang.

Most of them were peasants, and we know little of their lives except the outlines of the routines which farming imposed on them. Sometimes they appear in the designs on bronzes or as figures of clay, which give us some idea of their appearance, but most Chinese art concerned with men and women records the lives of the rich, well born and powerful. The peasants were not much touched by the Confucian beliefs of the upper classes and stuck to the superstitions of their own village and local gods and demons. Nonetheless there were some new religious beliefs which had a wide impact. Taoism, a development of primitive magic, was one, but the most important was Buddhism, which first reached China in about AD 64 and seems to have been regarded at first as a variant of Taoism.

Han pottery models of buildings. From the first century AD *onwards these were often placed in tombs.*

Pottery figures of acrobats, with musicians in the background.

American civilization

Whatever the contacts, large or small, between civilizations elsewhere, the one thing which is certain about the appearance of civilization in the Americas is that it owed nothing to the outside at all. The oceans isolated those continents, and within them big barriers of climate and topography hampered the spread of ideas and skills. They were occupied largely by peoples who never progressed beyond hunting and foraging. This was the situation of the 'Red' Indians, for example, encountered by Europeans who pushed into North America only a few centuries ago. They were Stone-Age peoples then suddenly confronted with the world of gunpowder.

Until modern times all the early stages of human development appear to have occurred later in the Americas than elsewhere. The most advanced area was for many centuries Central America; this was where agriculture first appeared. Because of differences of climate and botany, it took a different form from the agriculture of the Near East. One of the crucial early crops to be developed was maize – Indian corn, as it was later called – which began to be grown about 5000 BC and evolved in the next 3000 years into something like the plant we know today which gives us 'corn on the cob'. This happened first in Mexico, from which the plant spread southwards. Farther south potatoes and other starchy root vegetables were grown; together with squashes and various gourds they provided an increase in food production like that which had made larger populations possible elsewhere on the basis of cereal crops.

With farming came villages, weaving, pottery and a precivilized life similar to that found earlier elsewhere. All this was going on fairly soon after 2000 BC. About a thousand years later there appear the first signs of what has generally been recognized as the first American civilization, that of the Olmecs of eastern Mexico.

The Olmecs do not seem to have been literate, and in many ways their civilization fell short of those appearing elsewhere. Yet they had some remarkable achievements to their credit. In the first place, Olmec civilization lasted a long time (about six centuries) in the unpromising setting of the swampy forests of Central America, and it spread south as far as

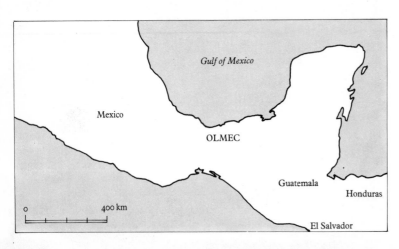

El Salvador. It was therefore vigorous enough
to find ways of dealing with local conditions. It
may have been that its inhabitants were
especially skilled at exploiting the possibilities
of quick growth offered by the jungle, by clearing and burning a patch of land, harvesting a
crop from it and then moving on. The destruction of archaeological evidence by the jungle
is so rapid that it is almost impossible to say
anything about Olmec settlements except
that the remains of their religious centres
are very impressive. They had large earth
pyramids (which must have required much
labour) and colossal sculpted monuments, to
say nothing of finely carved figures of jade at

the other end of the scale. Yet the Olmecs had
no metals.

Whatever the limitations of Olmec culture
it transmitted to later American civilizations
a legacy of great importance. The later gods
of Mexican peoples have been traced back to
the Olmec deities. The sites and plans of
Olmec temples are obviously connected in
some way with astronomical calculations, and
the ordering of the calendar began with them,
and was developed by later Americans. It
may also be that the pictographs of later
American peoples derive from Olmec origins,
though we have no evidence from Olmec
society itself about this.

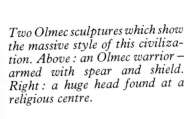

Two Olmec sculptures which show the massive style of this civiliza-tion. Above: an Olmec warrior – armed with spear and shield. Right: a huge head found at a religious centre.

Retrospect

There are no neat lines or dates dividing periods or ages when we are considering the history of the whole world. Somewhere early in the first millennium is a sensible place to break the story in the Aegean and Egypt, but the end of the Assyrian empire centuries later makes more sense in Mesopotamia. In India the age of the Buddha, and in China the Han empire, are helpful landmarks. This book therefore ends raggedly, at several places scattered across a zone of a thousand years or so.

By this time civilization had already made an irreversible difference to human life. Some of its effects went so deep that our lives are still being influenced by them. Prehistory is (except to prehistorians) the story of people who are all much the same: they have very limited possibilities open to them. With civilization, human variety becomes much more important and obvious. People still live in ways which clearly show the impact of such historical forces as Jewish religion, Babylonian mathematics, the Indian caste system and Confucian teaching (to take only a very few examples).

This may suggest that civilization is the story of the successful – or at least, of the influential – and indeed, in an important sense, this is true. But perhaps it is worth remembering at the very end of a book about how civilization appeared that great things were done even by peoples who did not achieve such cultural peaks, and that we ought not to overlook them in our proper admiration of what was done by those who arrived at and developed true civilization.

Consider for a moment the megaliths of prehistoric western Europe, the earliest of which were erected while the Near East was still on the way to literacy. The most splendid, but also younger, is Stonehenge, in southern England. It required the transport for many kilometres of huge blocks of stone and then their erection in a careful and exact pattern which is related to the rising of the sun at the summer solstice. Many of the other European megaliths – and they can be found all round the coasts of western Europe, from Malta, round Spain and Brittany, to the British Isles and Denmark – are simple tombs or standing stones ('dolmens'), but others are almost as

The purpose of the great megalithic constructions found over so
large an area of western Europe
is much debated. Left: at Car-
nac in Brittany nearly 3000
'menhirs' – single standing stones
–have been grouped and aligned
in multiple rows. At Castlerigg
(right) in northern England there
is a typical example of a stone
circle. The most elaborate site is
at Stonehenge (above) in southern England which seems to have
been laid out to allow observation
from within of the Midsummer
sunrise and Midwinter moonrise.

Building Stonehenge

It took six hundred years or so for Stonehenge to be finished and during this time techniques and skills were employed which were very advanced. We should not underrate the 'primitive' people who could carry out engineering on this scale and with the degree of accuracy shown in aligning the great stones. These operations must have been well-managed, which suggests that their arrangements of government were by no means simple tribal ones.

It seems that there have been not one but three Stonehenges. The first (top) consisted simply of a series of holes enclosed by a bank and a ditch, with entrance through a triple archway of timber. Later, stones, arranged in two circles, were erected in the centre, though this arrangement was never completed (middle). The bottom picture shows Stonehenge after the third and final rebuilding – this is basically the arrangement that survives today, though many of the stones have fallen.

elaborate as Stonehenge. They are sometimes laid out in patterns like groves or trees, and sometimes run in straight lines across country, perhaps for kilometres. Their purpose is unclear, but the careful alignment of the big groups seems to show that they are related to the movements of the sun, moon and stars and the passage of the seasons. This means that their builders knew a lot, at least in an informal way, about astronomy.

So impressive are these great monuments that it was once thought that the people who built them could only have done so after learning their art from the eastern Mediterranean, from Mycenae, perhaps, or from even farther east. This view is no longer held, though, for the latest radiocarbon estimates of the dates of these monuments do not fit the chronology of the old centres of civilization. It seems certain that, whatever contacts they had with one another's communities, the Europeans who built these strange works did so without stimulus or instruction from more advanced societies.

It is perfectly proper to decide that achievements on this scale are not the marks of a civilization, while the pyramids are. Certainly the societies which built them were not as complex and did not have as many other great achievements to their credit as did the inhabitants of the Nile. But the megalith-builders did marvellous things all the same and ought to be remembered for their own sake. Though the first civilizations dominate our picture of the ancient past, and though we owe so much to them, let our last thought be that they covered only a small part of the globe's surface. Many things which were interesting and important are liable to be lost sight of in the long shadows they cast.

The Hypogeum in Malta is a unique underground megolithic temple. Carved out of limestone rock, it consists of a labyrinth of halls and chambers on three distinct levels.

Time chart

BC

.3500 Europe: megalithic buildings, Neolithic farming cultures spread west. Lakeside village culture, Switzerland. Since c. 4500, copper mined and worked S.E. Europe (Vinca/Gumelnitsa culture). Chinese agriculture Yellow River: rice, millet, pigs domesticated. Nilotic agriculture. Egyptian trading ships in Mediterranean. Wheel invented Sumer. First writing, pictographic. Middle East

.3300 Era of first civilizations opens. Sumer (3300–200 BC); improvements in agriculture, metal-working, pottery, irrigation, glass-making, government, taxation, laws, cuneiform writing (c. 3200 BC)

.3200 Bronze casting in Near East
Unification of Upper and Lower Egypt

.3000 Use of decimal and sexagesimal (60) systems in Sumer (inc. fractions), first wheeled vehicles. Egyptian civilization: Old Kingdom – hieroglyphics, 365-day calendar, pyramids, wooden plough

.2500 Indus civilization: cities – Mohenjodaro, Harappa. Pictograph writing, cotton used, pottery, weaving, trading
Weights and measures used Egyptian, Indian and Mesopotamian civilizations. Bronze in use Egypt. Beaker Folk (so called because of characteristic pottery) introduced metal-working to many parts of Europe. China: irrigation, walled settlements

c.2400–2350 Akkad. Sargon I, first great emperor Near East, conquers Sumer
Britain: Stonehenge

c.2300 Beaker Folk settle in Britain, introduce metal-working China: wheel-turned pottery

c.2200 Akkad overthrown

c.2000 Indus civilization ends. Era of 'Aryan' invasions Sumerian civilization overthrown. Egyptians use sail-boats, ox-drawn plough. Bronze-casting widespread. Near East. Crete: Earliest building of palace at Knossos. Early Greek-speaking tribes settle Greece. Horse-drawn carts, N.E. Iran. China: Hsia period – silk, laquer, bronze, rice cultivated. Eskimo culture Bering Strait

c.1800 Mining and bronze casting in Austria

c.1740 Old Hittite Kingdom
Horses broken and ridden Central Asia

c.1700 Mycenaean civilization (to c. 1100)
Babylon. Hammurabi and his code of laws (c. 1750). Bronze Age in Britain. Early Greek settlements. Middle Minoan civilization: town life, Linear A script, Palace of Minos at Knossos rebuilt and enlarged. Chinese writing well established

c.1600 Hittites sack Babylon and flourish (to c. 1100 BC). Bronze Age, N. Italy. Mycenaeans conquer Crete. Late Minoan. Linear B script. Glassware first produced Babylon and Assyria. Beaker Folk mix with Indo-Europeans, Rhine Valley and Denmark

c.1500 Mycenaean civilization (c. 1100) flourishes. China: Shang Kingdom (to c. 1027 BC); advanced bronze technology, cities, jade, writing, pottery. Egypt: New Kingdom – Abu Simbel, medicine, literature, art India: Indo-European invasions. Aryans establish foundations of later Hindu civilization

c.1450 Earliest known writing in Greek language. Crete: Linear B

c.1400 Knossos finally destroyed. Phoenician alphabet (or earlier). First complete alphabet Ungarit people, Syria. Iron in use, Middle East

c.1250 Events remembered as Moses' leading of the Israelites from Egypt

c.1220–1210 Trojan War – Greeks destroy Troy

c.1200 The Sea Peoples ravage Aegean and Eastern Mediterranean. Camels domesticated Near East. Dorians invade Crete, introduce iron. Dorians destroy early settlements, Greece. Linear B script at Pylos and Mycenae

c.1100 Egypt: period of decline begins

c.1050 China: Chou Dynasty ousts Shang. Neo-Hittite and Aramaean kingdoms, N. Syria

c.1000 Iron Age, Near East, India. India: *Rig-Veda*, Sanskrit, bronze weapons. Phoenicians trade and flourish (to c. 700 BC). Saul first king of Israel. Africa: kingdoms of Nubia and Meroë. Reindeer domesticated N. Europe

c.935 Canaan divides: kingdoms of Israel and Judah

c.900 Etruscans first appear Italy. Celtic tribes in Germany. Phoenicians develop modern alphabet

c.885 Assyrian Empire. Nineveh

c.800 China: Warring States (to c. 221 BC): iron worked, irrigation, wheelbarrow invented. Etruscans settle central Italy (to c. 400 BC). First American civilizations – Olmecs on Gulf coast. Phoenicians found Carthage (c. 814 BC). Celtic culture spreads. Iron worked. Homer

776 Trad. date, first Olympic games

753 Trad. date, founding of Rome

c.750 Greek alphabet, adapted from Phoenician, spreads quickly

745–720 Assyrians conquer Neo-Hittite kingdoms, N. Syria

c.730 Ironwork in Meroë. Assyrians overrun Israel (c. 722 BC)

c.700 Greece: first coins, colonization, Athenian philosophy

c.671 Assyria conquers Egypt. Assyrian power at its peak

c.625 Neo-Babylonian (Chaldean) Empire, to c. 538 BC)

c.612 Fall of Nineveh. Assyrian Empire overthrown by Media and Babylon

c.600 Europe: Celtic (Hallstatt) Iron Age

c.587 Judah overrun by Babylonians

c.539 Persian Empire. Babylon captured by Cyrus (c. 539), Medes (c. 550), Lydia (c. 546). Achaemenian Empire (to c. 331 BC)

c.500 Rome a republic. Iron Age in Britain. India: rice cultivated, coins, writing

Acknowledgements

The author and publisher would like to thank the following for their kind permission to reproduce illustrative material: Ashmolean Museum for pp. 50 *below left* and 105 *above left* (Griffith Institute for p. 54 *above left*); Trustees of the British Museum for pp. 9, 16, 18 *right*, 19 *right*, 22, 40 *above* and *below right*, 42, 44 *both*, 46, 47 *above left*, 54 *centre left*, 58 *below*, 62 *below left*, 68 *below left*, 78 *left*, 82, 83, 86 *above*, 87, 91 *above*, 94, 103, *all* and 107 *above left*; Peter Clayton for p. 77 *below*; *Du Magazine* for p. 47 *below*; Robert Estall for p. 118; Faculty of Archaeology and Anthropology, Cambridge for p. 31 *centre*; Robert Harding Associates for pp. 2 *left*, 7 *below left*, 17, 33 *below left*, 36, 41 *above left*, and 112 *below*; D. A. Harissiadis for p. 91 *below*; Crown Copyright with permission of Controller of Her Majesty's Stationery Office for p. 120 *all*; John Hillelson Agency Ltd for pp. 7 *above*, 24 *above right*, 53 *below*, 59 *above right*, 60–61, 72 *both*, 78 *below right*, 81 and 88; Hirmer Fotoarchiv for pp. 20 *below left*, 58 *above left* and 95; Michael Holford for pp. 11 *below right*, 15 *above left*, 20 *above right*, 21 *above right*, 25 *below right*, 28 *left* and *below right*, 29 *above left*, 51, 53 *above*, 65 *above left*, 68 *above*, 73 *both*, 76 *below left*, 77 *above* and 85; Sean Hudson for p. 38; Ikon Library for p. 57; Iraq Petroleum Company Ltd for p. 18 *left*; Landesmuseum for p. 108; Liverpool Museum for p. 54 *above right*; Longman Group Ltd for p. 30; Louvre Museum for p. 70; Macquity International Collection for pp. 21 *below left*, 32, 112 *above right* and 115 *both*; Macdonald Educational for p. 37 *below*; Metropolitan Museum of Art for p. 71; National Archaeological Museum, Athens for pp. 3 *right* and 93 *above left*, *below right* and *below left*; National Museum, New Delhi for p. 33 *above left*; Nelson Gallery – Atkins Museum, Kansas City, Missouri (Nelson Fund) for p. 54 *below right*; Oriental Institute, Chicago for p. 19 *left*; Pennsylvania University Museum for pp. 8 *both*, 21 *above left* and 62 *above left*; Diana Phillips for pp. 92 *left* and 93 *above left*; Photoresources for pp. 15 *below*, 40 *left*, 41 *below left*, 45 *right*, 48, 49, 58 *right*, 62 *right*, 64 *both*, 68 *right*, 76 *right*, 96 *both*, 97 *left*, 109, 111 and 119 *above*; Popperfoto for pp. 11 *left*, 27 *above*, 31 *left* and *right*, 102, 105 *centre left* and 117 *right*; Photo: Science Museum for p. 55; Ronald Sheridan for pp. 24 *below*, 65 *right*, 92 *right*, 97 *below* and 101 *below*; Skira for pp. 52 *below right* (photograph by Claudio Emmer) and 69 *above right*; *The Sunday Times* for p. 28 *above right*; Syndication International for p. 107 *above right*; Peter Tucker for p. 39 *left*; Turin Archaeological Museum for p. 52 *above left*; Wellcome Medical Institute for p. 45 *left*; Werner Forman Archive for pp. 3 *left*, 20 *below right*, 41 *right*, 52 *below left*, 57 *right*, 105 *above right* and *below right* and *below left* and 117 *left*; Roger Wood for pp. 23 *right*, 24 *above left*, 25 *left*, 29 *below*, 50 *right*, 52 *above right*, 56, 99 *both*, 100 *both*, 101 *above* and 104.

The author and publishers would like to thank the following illustrators for the maps and diagrams: Ray and Corinne Burrows for pp. 36 *below*, 37 *above*, 43, 86 *below*, 92 *above right* and 120 *left*; Michael Craig for pp. 74–5; Vana Haggerty for pp. 17 *below*, 21 *below right* and 27 *below*; Illustra for p. 30 *left*; Kathleen King for pp. 6, 12, 22 *above*, 34, 66, 79 *above*, 80, 82 *left*, 83 *below*, 84, 88 *below*, 90, 94 *above*, 98, 107 *below*, 113, 116 and 121 *above*; Arthur Lockwood for pp. 13 and 44 *above left*; Helena Zakrzewska-Rucinska for pp. 59 *above left*, 67 *above*, 69 *left*, 71 *left* and *below right* and 99 *right*.

Index